My Truthful and Life Changing Stories

Jackie Dee Cunningham

ISBN 978-1-66785-488-5

Printed in USA by BookBaby

www.bookbaby.com

To my wife, Judy, forever and always

Table of Contents

Table of Contents (cont'd)

Acknowledgments

Throughout my life, various people have watched over and guided me in different endeavors. I call these people angels.

My wife inspired me to write this book and has been instrumental from the very beginning in encouraging its completion. Thank you, Susan Howell, for editing the book. You sorted through a lot of correspondence, from me to you, over there on the West Coast. Thank you, Sylvia Whitmore, for leading me to an eventual publisher. Judy Horsley Hughes, thanks for reminding me to finish what I started. Ladies, your input and support have been integral to getting this project completed. Thank you all, once again.

Introduction

While sometimes posting personal stories on social media and telling stories at social gatherings, various people have said they would like to read my book. Over the years, I began writing and collecting some of these stories.

After a good bit of deliberation over whether to write a novel, whether to write in third person, and how to go about compiling a book, I decided just to write the way that I speak. A few corrections and clean ups seem to have left my particular vernacular still intact, so here it is. Hope you enjoy!

Chapter 1

(My Mother)

Mamie Frances Tyree was one of sixteen children born to poor and uneducated parents. Looking back, I realize she had a handicap, but at first sight appeared normal until she spoke. Then it was instantly realized there was a problem.

Reading and writing were problematic for her, and she would struggle for most of her life with simple tasks. If food didn't come in a can, there would not be a meal on the table.

She was put to work early in life helping her father and siblings in the wood cutting business. It mattered little if it was cold or hot outside. The hard work was necessary to feed and clothe so many children.

Even though she was a reasonably good-looking girl who attracted intelligent men at times, relationships would also be problematic for her for the rest of her life. I'm convinced she was sought after and easily taken advantage of by various men.

My birth took place on July 28,1948, in Gladstone, VA, in a modest country house owned by her sister. The house sat on a hillside at the end of a red dirt road. My mother was eighteen and unwed at the time.

There was no doctor or anyone with professional, medical experience in attendance. According to my mother, there was trouble with my delivery, and I was unhealthy for some time after birth.

Miraculously, I improved, and even though future life was hard, I had a smile on my face and enthusiasm in my heart. This was natural and a gift from God. I firmly believe that.

It would be seven years after my birth before a birth certificate was finally obtained from the Virginia Department of Health Office of Vital Statistics in Richmond, Virginia. It did not list any information relating to my birth date or even my mother's full name. It simply said Forrest Peyton Tyree, the date of issue, and my mother's maiden name Tyree on another line.

My mother could not return to her home with a child, and finally, one of the men she was seeing took her to his home. They moved into a smokehouse that had multiple salt-cured hams hanging from the first-floor ceiling. They slept with me on the second floor. Of course, I don't remember this, but I do love salt-cured country ham, to this day, for some reason.

It was not long before this man who had taken my mother and me in, under threat from my mother's family, married my mother just in time for her to give birth to a second child. It was later confirmed through DNA testing that my sister and I were not the biological children of this man she married. It was evident after our births that we were not his children. We did not remotely favor the man.

We eventually moved from the smokehouse into a small three-room house that hastily had been erected for the growing number of people in this group. I would not refer to it as a family.

I was about three at the time that this new house was built. And it was becoming abundantly clear that I was not being accepted into this household because I was thought to be the son of my stepfather's first cousin.

My great-grandmother and great-aunt lived on the adjacent close hillside, and I began to walk over to visit them. It was not long before they just kept me with them. They, of course, were aware of my unpopularity in the house my mother and her husband were living in.

I was content and loved by these two ladies and paid little attention to what went on in my mother's house.

12

These two ladies protected me and taught me the Bible by reading stories to me. And they saw to it I was fed. I even slept between them. They gave me strength that they knew I would need in life.

In the next two years, my mother would give birth to two more children. It is firmly believed that their father was my mother's current husband.

Another romance was looming soon for my mother when she met a man who was really interested in her sister. Sparks flew as they began an affair that eventually broke up her marriage to my stepfather. She had now become pregnant by a fourth man in the neighborhood.

A divorce took place and my stepfather moved into the house I was living in. This was not good for me. In fact, his moving in with us was very traumatic.

Because of my three siblings, my mother was allowed to remain in the house that was built after leaving the smokehouse. But even that did not last long.

Things began to turn from bad to awful as my stepfather increasingly began to drink and would visit my mother. She rejected his advances because she was totally smitten with her new lover.

Once, when my older sister and I were walking through the woods coming home from school, we were shot at by our stepfather. He later claimed that he thought we were our mother's lover. My sister confronted him about this event after she became an adult.

It was not long after that event that my mother just picked up and left one day, leaving behind three children so she could be near her new love's family. But her boyfriend was stopped soon afterwards by a state trooper.

The trooper had noticed that there was a billy goat in the back seat of the car the boyfriend was driving. The goat had his head out of the window. I am assuming he was enjoying fresh air.

During the stop, the trooper realized that the driver was wanted for larceny and was arrested along with the man accompanying him. The billy goat was not charged with anything and was returned to its owner.

Soon after this case went to trial, the judge ordered both men to serve time in the Virginia State Penitentiary in Richmond. My mother's lover, now the father of her latest child, decided that perhaps if they were married, the judge would lessen the time he would spend in prison.

The plan did not work, but at least my mother was married again and was able to bring subsequent children into the world legitimately. In all, my mother had seven children by four different men.

My three deserted siblings were rescued and brought to live with my great-aunt and me. My great-grandmother had passed away by this time.

My stepfather, his brother, and their uncle also lived with us. There were now four adults and four children living in the house.

I was now almost seven, and my youngest sibling was four. The four of us children slept in the same bed, and at times, we all four would wet the bed. It was not pleasant. We also shared this same room with my great-aunt.

My great-aunt had both physical and mental issues and had been placed in a mental hospital on several occasions. My stepfather's uncle was crippled and needed crutches to walk.

Of course, my stepfather and his brother worked day jobs. That left my siblings and me to the job of taking care of ourselves. We fed ourselves when we could find food in the house. This was mostly light bread, cereal, butter, and sugar.

And if we were lucky, when one of the adults was not feeling well or was just plain sick, there would be orange juice, fruit, and prunes, and sometimes grapes. We would throw caution to the wind and naturally gobble it up. We were hungry.

Most of our clothes were made by hand by my great-aunt and some neighbors. Even though my great-aunt had problems, she managed to help the four of us as best she could.

There was coldness towards me from time to time, as the burden of taking care of the four of us was taking its toll on the breadwinners. After all, my sister and I were not my stepfather's children.

One day, I had taken something that I should not have taken, and out of the clear blue, I saw my stepfather walking towards me with a stick in his hand. He grabbed me and beat me until I could not stand up to walk.

He beat me in my private area, and I was bleeding on multiple parts of my body from head to toe. Thank God my sister was close by and stood between me and the attack. I was semi-conscious and just lay in the yard for a while until I could gain some strength to move.

Sometime later, my stepfather came towards me again, and I stood my ground and yelled and told him that he was not my father and that he had no right to hurt me anymore. He stopped his aggressive behavior that day and never touched me again. I always knew he was not my biological father, because my mother had told me this many times whenever he was mean to me.

Several people had called me a red headed (insert biological father's name) looking son of a bitch. My grandfather had even chased me across a cornfield with a whip and fired a shotgun in the air to scare me when I was about five years old, and at the same time, he was cussing at me. It worked. But I had done nothing to merit this bad treatment.

The four of us kids were treated well when we had people in the neighborhood volunteering to help us with meals, bathing, and clothes. Some were even paid to watch after us from time to time. My biological grandmother would come to help with the situation sometimes too. But she and I never were close, even though she would take me to church occasionally.

She was so ashamed of the relationship that her son had had with my mother. That relationship brought me into this world. I would pay for it for the rest of her life.

-Gladstone Elementary-

I suppose even children who hate school can remember a favorite story or two from early school years. I started Gladstone Elementary School on Route 60 at age seven. The building currently houses the Gladstone Rescue Squad.

This school had six grades. First, second, and third were taught in one room. Fourth, fifth, and sixth were taught in the second room.

Students had an advantage of sorts, because they could hear what was being taught in the next grade level. I remember watching a second grader write on the blackboard the numbers from one to one hundred, and I was in awe as a first grader.

When I was finally in the third grade, I remember sitting beside a much bigger boy wearing overalls. He appeared to have a slight mustache. I believe he was much older than me. I think he must have quit school because I didn't see him in the fourth grade.

We could buy lunch or bring our lunch to school, and somehow my lunch was paid for. The food was good, or at least it was to me.

Our cook, in the school kitchen, made coleslaw with celery seeds as part of our lunch. I had never tasted anything like it before. It took me a few years to figure out what celery seeds were, since I had never even heard of celery.

I remember having a crush on a girl in the fourth grade. By the time lunch was over, I was so hooked on the new food taste that I had forgotten about the crush. That was the one and only time that I ever allowed that memory slip.

In 1958, in the fourth grade, my teacher was Mrs. Parrish, who was a strong disciplinarian but very fair. I liked her.

There were times in the 50s when my siblings and I often went to school hungry. Hunger was not unusual for many other kids either. Rarely did we have food items that we desired and needed.

The Nelson County school system had a contract with Monticello Dairy in Charlottesville. The dairy items were delivered to the school in Monticello delivery trucks.

I knew very well what items could be found on these trucks. When I had money, I purchased their ice cream and chocolate milk from the school freezer that was located in our classroom.

One morning, I was playing with other kids behind the school when the dairy delivery truck arrived. As soon as the driver entered the small cafeteria, I did something that was not planned at all.

I had a vision that prompted me to leap, out of the clear blue, onto the rear bumper of the truck and open the heavy door. This would allow me to enter the milk storage area and hopefully grab a container of chocolate milk and exit the truck. That vision of enjoying that cold, awesome tasting chocolate milk vanished quickly, and I had another vision.

The next vision I had was of me freezing to death inside the refrigerated area of the truck. The heavy door slammed shut right when I entered the milk area because of the way the truck was parked.

Realizing my dilemma did not require me to be a gifted child. I was going to be caught inside the locked milk compartment of the truck when the driver returned. Secondly, Mrs. Parrish was not going to be a happy camper when this event was reported to her.

I'm not sure exactly how long I was trapped inside the truck. It couldn't have been too long. I had not yet frozen to death, when I saw daylight, as the driver opened the heavy door. He had to have heard my pounding on the door and my loud screaming.

If I had not panicked as I did, it would have been an outstanding time to actually pray for deliverance. Nonetheless, this is a wonderful opportunity to give God credit for my escape. Thank you, Lord. Sorry I'm sixty-four years late.

I was physically taken to Mrs. Parrish by the driver. She was a very understanding lady.

I received a very sound talking to, and that probably hurt worse than a spanking, if the truth be told, because I respected her. She knew it, and she respected me back that day.

Yes, I still love chocolate milk and anything else that has chocolate. And I never had another vision of taking milk from the Monticello milk truck!

-The Fable-

Persuasion is better than force, in most cases. I applied this thinking throughout my life, and I believe it worked.

My first, second, and third grade teacher at Gladstone was Mrs. Sites. I will always remember her sharing famous literature with our classes. She was indeed a lovely lady.

The North Wind & the Sun

The North Wind and the Sun had a quarrel about which of them was the stronger. While they were disputing with much heat and bluster, a Traveler passed along the road wrapped in a cloak.

"Let us agree," said the Sun, "that he is the stronger who can strip that Traveler of his cloak."

"Very well," growled the North Wind, and at once sent a cold, howling blast against the Traveler.

With the first gust of wind the ends of the cloak whipped about the Traveler's body. But he immediately wrapped it closely around him, and the harder the Wind blew, the tighter he held it to him. The North Wind tore angrily at the cloak, but all his efforts were in vain.

Then the Sun began to shine. At first his beams were gentle, and in the pleasant warmth after the bitter cold of the North Wind, the Traveler unfastened his cloak and let it hang loosely from his shoulders. The Sun's rays grew warmer and warmer. The man took off his cap and mopped his brow. At last he became so heated that he pulled off his cloak, and, to escape the blazing sunshine, threw himself down in the welcome shade of a tree by the roadside.

Gentleness and kind persuasion win where force and bluster fail.

–Aesop, author-

(Winter, Library of Congress)

Chapter 2

(The Children's Home)

Thank God it was decided that the four of us would be sent to a children's home in Salem, Virginia. We were taken, along with my grandmother, to Richmond, by Pastor Kirby of Mineral Springs Baptist Church. An evaluation and IQ test would be given before the children's home would accept us.

Sometime later, when the results were known and my IQ score was the highest of the four of us, it naturally made my stepfather mad, and he let me know it. But at least he didn't hit me.

It was soon afterwards, in August of 1959, that we were driven to the Virginia Baptist Children's Home and turned over to the staff. We were not shown any affection from my grandmother as she and the pastor drove off. I was eleven.

We dreaded the transfer from the start. And it proved to be that way for most of my stay. Immediately upon arrival and removing what little clothing we had from the preacher's car, as well as my homemade wagon, it became noticeably clear to me that this was not to be a happy place for me.

With all our belongings sitting on the ground, someone talked to my grandmother for a few minutes. Then the four of us were taken to our cottages, and we were left alone with complete strangers. The only people we knew in Salem had just abruptly driven away.

My two sisters were both taken to the same cottage. My brother and I were taken to Carpenter Cottage.

After being assigned a room and a bed, I was free to walk around the campus and to acclimate myself to the new environment. It didn't take but a few minutes of this activity to realize that would not happen, at least, not on this particular day. Being the new kid, seeking some sort of friendly gesture, meant nothing to anyone else.

As I stepped onto the porch of a cottage, just down the sidewalk from Carpenter Cottage, a larger boy approached me, pushed me off the porch and said, "Don't come back to my cottage." He and I would later become distant friends, but I never forgot his ugliness to me on my first day and never really ever trusted him.

After being pushed off the porch, I grabbed my homemade wagon and started pulling my brother around the immediate area of our cottage until the kids started making fun of the wagon and us. Naturally, we returned to our cottage and just went inside and sat on our beds.

The cottage had a TV, and I wanted to go to the TV room. But I was so intimidated by the past few minutes of unpleasant behaviors that I stayed in my assigned room. I would soon share this room with at least six other children.

After a few days, my brother and I relaxed a little as we were becoming more accepted by the other children. My two sisters, however, never thought they had a friend during their stay.

One of the first people that I actually talked to, who seemed to be eager to learn about me, was a boy from Lynchburg named James. We began hanging around together along with my brother.

We were expected to keep our living areas clean. On each Saturday, everyone spent most of the morning scrubbing, waxing, and buffing the floors with a huge buffer that we all would seek to operate. Later we would be assigned to work on the farm gathering potatoes, corn, and feeding and milking our milk cows.

When my brother and I were placed into Carpenter Cottage, I realized very early on that there was a strange tree on the side of it. I would later learn it was a pecan tree.

Having never heard of pecans before 1959 and not knowing what they tasted like, I inquired about the many pecans that grew on the tree. They were also lying all over the ground. I learned that they were safe to eat. And eat I did!

I fell completely in love with pecans and ate them almost daily. Realizing that other kids liked them as well, I devised a plan to always have them available to me.

Using an old shoe box and empty jars, as well as other types of containers, I began my quest to always have an abundance of pecans available and to fill everything I could get my hands on to store them.

They were hidden under my bed at first, but soon afterwards, others began taking my pecans. So, I began hiding them in bushes and other hiding places I deemed safe.

Well, it was not long before everybody soon figured it all out and began calling me "Squirrel." I am known by several different names in different locations, but in Salem and at the June reunions we have every year, I am still called Squirrel.

Even though I had not been in a physical fight in my life, thus far, it was inevitable that it would happen in an environment such as this, with so many children at the home. Approximately half of the two hundred plus children were boys.

My first confrontation began in a rather nice setting, as I, along with my new and only friend James, went to the Salem theater just a short walking distance from the children's home. Upon arrival, I noticed my sister and her friend Brenda were sitting in front of James and me.

I did not know Brenda very well, but I did know that James liked her. I paid little attention to her and was only interested in watching the movie. This was a new experience for me since I never had been to a theater until living in Salem.

During the movie, my sister Marjorie got up and walked to where James and I were sitting. She invited me alone to sit with Brenda. Brenda had shared with my sister that she liked me but was too bashful to ask me herself.

Well before I could process the invitation, James got up and struck me with his fist, causing my nose to bleed. He scared the devil out of me because James was somewhat older and a little bigger than me.

It didn't take me long to decide what to do. I got up and left the movie. I walked back to the children's home because I was afraid I was going to cry and knew that fighting James would not end well for me.

I had no idea that James was such a mean kid, and I was completely caught off guard. This whole event was extremely embarrassing, and I was uncertain of myself for sure.

After Mrs. Smith, my housemother, saw my bloody clothes and heard my explanation, she and another older boy who lived in our cottage punished James. I would not have said anything to her if she had not seen me when I arrived at my cottage.

Sometime later, James attacked my little brother Richard who also lived in our cottage. Since Richard was younger than James and me, I knew that action on my part was required. Fearing James, I was by no means looking forward to it. I did not want to bleed again.

Well, I pondered the situation for a day or so and planned my course of action. I had recently been given a soprano ukulele, and of course, I could not make it sound like anything enjoyable to listen to. But I decided the sound of music was not what I had in mind and did not require James to enjoy hearing the music but "feel" the music instead.

I approached James and explained that I was just learning to play this beautiful instrument and would appreciate him walking with me behind the cottage to listen to my new talent in providing music. James somehow agreed, and off we went. I did not want to attack him where people could see just in case he got the best of me and humiliated me once again.

Once we were behind the cottage, I strummed the ukulele a few times and noticed that James was not appreciating my talent in strumming. So, I put into place my intended purpose, which was to surprise him with a forceful blow to his head, using my ukulele.

I knew not to overlook the fact that I had to use the element of surprise and be very thorough in inflicting as much pain as I could to disorient him and prevent him from gaining the upper hand. It worked.

After I felt that James was not going to respond in an unpleasant way towards me, I shared with James a few minutes of sound advice. It appeared he was still capable of hearing, or at least, his demeanor suggested it.

My instruction to him was very plain and to the point. I said, "Do not touch my brother ever again," and I took for granted that he understood that message would include me as well. James was a changed young man after this event, and I was very relieved to witness a new awakening of peace and goodwill within his heart towards my little brother and me.

Later in life, around 1974, I came across James on Campbell Avenue in Lynchburg. He lived in a trailer park just off the street, and it was obvious that James had not fared well in life.

It brought me to tears, and I was trying to hide my sympathy for him. I offered to give him money or to help in any way I could, but he refused.

I felt so bad that he appeared to not understand that what I did to him was not in my heart. But rather, protection of my little brother was what I had in mind. James died a short time later as a very young man, and tears fill my eyes as I finish this story.

School had started soon after our arrival at the home, and we felt out of place, as each morning, our teachers would require all the children from both the Virginia Baptist Children's Home and the Lutheran Children's Home of the South to raise their hands so we could receive our red and blue lunch tickets. The Lutheran children's home was a few miles from the Baptist children's home.

We were made to be conspicuous again. But I finally became used to it and didn't care anymore.

I started Broad Street Elementary School in the fifth grade and failed. I had to repeat the fifth grade at the beginning of the next school year in 1960. I had little interest in school and often asked God to never allow me to like the home or this school.

To this day, it's awfully hard for me to realize just what happened to me once I left Gladstone. Even though I had been mistreated and my feelings had been hurt so many times, it seemed that somehow my adjustment to such treatment had offered me an acceptance of it. It's hard to say.

But I do know that my new environment in Salem, at times, was very exciting, and it was so much fun seeing and experiencing new things. Still, it felt strange, and I withdrew into myself without an interest in anything positive. Applying myself in school was out of the question.

The children's home became very concerned and sent me to different medical professionals to try to determine what had happened to me. I actually enjoyed talking to the psychiatrists because it led to the release of so many emotional issues. But the release did not motivate me to improve my desire to stay in school.

Virginia Baptist Children's Home always did everything in its power to help me grow into a functional adult. We had good meals, medical care as needed, and plenty of physical activity. Nothing regarding my care could explain my attitude. And ample developmental opportunities were presented to the children as much as possible.

Now, as an adult, my own assessment of my problem, at that time, was that my soul was devoid of any feelings of real happiness. My soul was instead filled with feelings of being humiliated, unwanted, and abandoned. This left me without any self-confidence whatsoever.

Years later, after reading a letter sent to my grandmother, from my children's home caseworker, it was obvious that the caseworker had identified a part of my problem when she stated, "Forrest will never forgive his mother for what happened to him."

After I had read that old letter, it brought back thoughts that I had truly experienced. The caseworker was right. At one point, I considered ending my life and thinking, "I hope my mother cries when I am dead."

After about a year and a half in Carpenter Cottage, my first housing area, I was moved to Elliot Cottage, the next cottage just down the sidewalk from where I was. This was the cottage where I was pushed off the porch when I first arrived. The boy who pushed me still lived in the building. Fortunately, it was not a problem since we worked on the farm together and got along fairly well.

It was during this time that an unusual event took place that made me aware of what good things were in store for the future. Two college girls moved into one of the rooms just across from my room. They were in training, for the summer, for future work in children's social services. This is what I thought as there was no other valid reason I could think of for them being there.

The two young women spent time talking to us, and at times, they watched TV with us in the downstairs area. It was during one of those times that they were sitting behind me, and one had her feet in the empty chair beside me.

For some unknown reason, I reached over and picked her feet up and placed them in my lap, at which point I started massaging them. This went on for several minutes until the TV show was over and we all got up to leave.

As we reached the bottom of the stairs, just outside the TV room door, the girl I had been massaging threw her arms around my neck and began kissing me like I had never been kissed before. I was a quick learner and responded in kind.

It was at this time that her friend tried to separate us and eventually did. I remember the logical one telling the girl that kissed me, "You can't do that." Well, I disagreed wholeheartedly, but unfortunately, my vote did not count.

I must say my imagination was indeed triggered. But this never happened again, and we would only smile at each other in passing. I noticed that she did not sit next to or behind me again in the TV room.

I rarely saw my two sisters, who lived across the campus from where I was. I only saw them in the dining hall at mealtime. My brother was in a different building as well, and every effort was made by his housemother to keep us apart. She deemed me to be a bad influence on him. I simply just gave up the effort and moved around with the few friends I had.

It was not long before all three of my siblings were in foster homes. Eventually, all three were adopted by couples who were unable to have children of their own.

I know it sounds strange, but I never paid any attention to the adoptions at all until my siblings were gone. My life was unhappy and hectic at times with milking cows, loading hay from the fields, picking up potatoes, and working on the pig farm. And when I was not doing required work at the children's home, I would do yard work and shovel snow for pay when people in the town of Salem needed that sort of work done.

My need for money began early in life as I washed my own clothes and purchased my own shirts and trousers when I had enough money to do so. When I was attending school, it was obvious that my clothes were lacking in style and newness, and I sought to remedy that.

Very rarely did I have visitors from home and never did my stepfather or my grandmother ever visit. There were times my mother would show up with whoever would bring her. It often embarrassed me as the people who provided transportation for her were drinking alcohol or driving old, dirty cars. But I tried to put on a happy face and made the best of it.

In late 1962, I was moved once again to a new cottage named English Cottage that had a housemother who was particularly good to me. Her name was Ms. Hayes. Later on, after I left the children's home, she played a part in my life for which I will be forever grateful.

On a few occasions, I'd get rather unique opportunities to shine. One such occasion was when VBCH played basketball against Greenbrier Military School, Lewisburg, WVA.

I was not even considered a second-string player. I was a bench warmer.

Things were not going well for us. The coach looked at me with pity and said, "Squirrel, get ready to go in."

I was nervous. Somehow, I got the ball a few seconds later and I heard the coach hollering at me, "Pass the ball! Pass the ball!" He didn't believe that I could make a bucket while standing on a ladder.

Well, I knew that this was going to be in all likelihood my only chance for stardom. I threw the ball at the goal.

I turned to walk towards the bench not even looking to see where the ball went after I threw it. Then there was a small applause.

The ball had gone into the basket. I took my place on the bench knowing that I had played my game this night and not the team's. That was not the way it was to be done as a team player. I went to the shower room after the game and got dressed, leaving behind my basketball shoes, and until now, the memory of finally scoring a basket.

Chapter 3

(Christmas)

A Christmas I will never forget is one when Saint Nick did not show up! While living in the Virginia Baptist Children's Home in the 50s and 60s, Christmas was sometimes okay. But most of the time, it was a very unhappy holiday for me as well as for some of the other children who lived at the home.

Those children who still had family who were interested in them would usually leave for the holidays with a family member. Various people throughout Virginia, who were interested in helping children, might also come pick up a child and take them to their homes for the holidays. My two sisters and a brother had already been adopted, so I was the only one of my family left in Salem.

While living at the children's home for those five years, I never went to be with any of my family members for Christmas, but I was invited to share one Christmas with a family in Roanoke. It was the worst experience you could imagine, since I did not know the people, and I possessed no money to enable me to buy them gifts in return for those given to me. This family was very generous.

I felt extremely uncomfortable at the dinner table as this family and their grown children were trying to make me feel a part of their happiness. It was not working! But I did appreciate their effort.

Had it not been for Brook Benton, Dinah Washington, and a host of other popular singers in the 60s who could be heard singing on the small transistor radio I had acquired, it would have been much worse. I went to a bedroom at that home and closed the door as I sought to retreat and just be left alone. The situation was so awkward that I wanted to be returned to the children's home and left completely alone there, where I knew the territory and other kids that were left alone at Christmas.

From that point on, I refused to ever again be given sympathy from people I did not know, particularly at Christmas time. I decided that I would just stay at the children's home during the holidays and often stayed in a cottage alone.

I remember my friend, John, would come to where I was to check on me from time to time. John lived in the cottage next to mine.

The next Christmas came, and true to my word, I stayed in my cottage with a few others who either had no place to go, or like me, didn't want to go. On Christmas Eve, I was selected with another young boy to go to the supply room to pick up gifts to distribute to the few cottages that had children in them. We were to deliver these gifts to the housemothers in charge of each cottage.

We each had different cottages to deliver to. After delivering all the gifts that had been tagged for each child who was present, I was eager to return to my cottage to see what my gift would be, since we were allowed to open gifts on Christmas Eve.

Upon entering my cottage, after finishing my deliveries and looking under the small Christmas tree that had been put up, I noticed that there were no gifts under the tree. While I was on the other side of the campus, the children in my cottage had received gifts from the other delivery boy and had opened their gifts in advance of my returning to my cottage.

Nobody was in the sitting area where the tree was, since all children and the housemother were in the basement watching TV and playing games. It dawned on me that somehow my name had been overlooked as the gifts had been prepared for every child with no place to go that was left on campus.

To say that I felt bad would not come close to explaining the pain and disappointment that I felt. At this point, I knew that I would not mention this to my housemother or staff, since I felt so left out and very hurt by this omission, and I did not want to bring unwanted attention to myself. This was something that I had to bear alone to keep my feelings hidden, since I did not feel comfortable with anyone observing my pain.

The hurt was so real that I simply walked back outside into the mild snowstorm we were having and looked across the campus. Then I looked up into the dark sky and just let the snowflakes fall gently on my face to hide my tears, as they flowed from my eyes, just in case someone came along. And somehow, after contemplating suicide for a very brief moment, I decided from inner strength that I never knew I possessed to simply go back inside and turn my transistor radio on. My hopes were of hearing Brook Benton and Dinah Washington sing in perfect harmony, as I drifted off to sleep.

Years later, at one of our reunions, a friend told a story about a Christmas that made me feel a little better. He said that he had received a girls' doll as his gift and was also hurt and ashamed to say anything about it, since he felt like they did not even remember he was a boy.

Sometimes, life is hard and almost unbearable at times, and we all have a desire to be loved, wanted, and acknowledged. The best cure, for the lack of caring feelings from others, is to give love or help to someone who is hurting, making them feel appreciated, even if you don't know them.

It's amazing how much better you will feel when you detect a smile on someone's face that didn't know they were going to smile that day. And it's amazing how much better you will feel, knowing that you were responsible for someone lonely or hurting to feel better. I still love to hear Brook Benton and Dinah Washington sing!

Chapter 4

(My New Name)

After my three siblings had been adopted, and I was moved to English Cottage, I was lonely and rarely received mail from home, and I never had any visitors. The children's home had tried on two different occasions to place me with families who wanted to adopt a young male child. It just did not work. I was determined not to refer to anyone, other than my real mother and stepfather, as mother or father.

After my oldest sister had been adopted by a family in Lawrenceville, Virginia, she set out to find a family for me as well. I was not aware of this, at the time, and had no interest in the possibility of it. But one weekend, my sister and her new family came to see me, and they brought another man and woman with them from Lawrenceville.

The woman worked in a dentist's office where Marjorie had dental work done, and as Marjorie was leaving the office, she mentioned me to this lady. This lady and her husband had a daughter together, but the daughter was leaving home soon.

After talking to my sister, the couple decided to explore the possibility of adoption. Marjorie told the woman that she would like to introduce her and her husband to me.

The folks were genuinely nice, and we all went out to lunch and got to know each other. I really did not know what was going on, and they asked if I would like to visit their home. At the same time, I could spend some time with my sister.

I agreed. Within several weeks, they reappeared at the children's home to pick me up for the visit. Of course, all of this was being done with the cooperation of the children's home staff. It was summertime, and I had complete freedom to ride my bike around the area of their small home, located just outside the Lawrenceville town limits.

Sometimes I would accompany the man, who was a painter, to his jobs and even began to help. No pressure was put on me to do so. I just chose to help.

Everything was going very well. Towards the end of summer, the couple asked if I would like to remain with them since they wanted to adopt me. They wanted to start the paperwork before school started in the fall.

Personally, I really missed the few friends I had made at the home in Salem and really had a hard time agreeing to it. But finally, I did.

Several weeks passed when one evening, the couple informed me that even though I was going by the name Forrest Peyton Cunningham, my name was actually Forrest Peyton Tyree. Because I was born out of wedlock, I was given my mother's family name.

Everybody assumed that my name was Cunningham because my mother had married my stepfather, a Cunningham. That was not the case.

At the time of my birth, I was not registered with the Virginia Department of Vital Statistics in Richmond because I was not born in a hospital. And no one thought to take care of it until time to enter the first grade, when a birth certificate would be required.

It would be 1955, at age seven, before I would have anything resembling a birth certificate. That was the year I began school in Nelson County at Gladstone Elementary.

Well in Gladstone, not everything was done according to state regulations and rules, and due to the ineptness of those with any authority over me and the lack of concern for me, it was never a real issue to correct my name. No one in my estimation ever thought about it or cared one way or the other.

Finally, my grandmother stepped in and decided she had better get a grip on this situation, in a hurry, because her son was my biological father. Heaven forbid if the world found out somehow!

She never liked me and was ashamed that her son had fathered a child out of wedlock, particularly with my mother. She had no respect for my mother.

Back in Lawrenceville, after I found out about my true legal name, I remember getting up from that small kitchen table and requesting, with all the earnestness and sincerity that I could muster, to be taken back to Salem to the children's home. I wanted to leave right away. The folks informed me that I would have to wait until the next day, which I did.

We arrived back in Salem about mid-day. After getting resituated in my room after being away, I took off for the director's office. The secretary, to my great disappointment, said he had left for the day. I was determined to see him the following morning and resolved to do so.

So, the next day, I approached the huge administration building. This building was always like a "magic castle" to the children. It was an incredible structure which housed apartments, offices, a laundry area, and even a chapel. The architecture was amazing to me. And to the dismay of many, it was torn down many years later.

There were two young couples sitting on the steps of the building. I vaguely remembered the two young boys but did not know either of the young girls. Nevertheless, I immediately made eye contact and a connection with one of the girls. She did seem familiar.

I ran up the steps and to the director's office. I explained to him how I felt. And I didn't have to say much, since the way I felt was quite obvious.

I was crying and shaking all over and was barely able to talk. The director calmed me down and suggested that he would help me change my name to Cunningham if my previous stepfather were agreeable. But I was not finished with my wish.

I continued to explain that I wanted to change ALL my name so no one would mistake me for a Tyree. Any possible connection that could be made by accident or recollection, or anything, on anybody's part, gravely concerned me.

The director thought for a moment or two and asked me if I was sure. I responded, "Yes," quickly, without any room for misunderstanding and he said, "OK." I was told to produce a name that I would be happy with and then come back and talk to him.

This administrator was a particularly good man to me the whole time that I was at the children's home and never once gave me any well-deserved spankings at any time during my five years on campus. However, he did not allow me back, later on, due to one specific runaway issue, which I'll speak of later.

Exiting the building, I noticed the young girl I had made eye contact with earlier. Brenda and I began talking to each other, hitting it right off. It would not be long before she and I started a close friendship. In fact, Brenda and I became an inseparable couple for the next two years until I again would leave the children's home. But we remained friends until the time she passed away. Our friendship endured for fifty-nine years.

At this time, I was assigned to Boys Memorial Cottage to share a room with a boy I knew, but not well. As I unpacked my belongings to settle down on campus, once again I confided in my roommate my dilemma and asked him to help me choose a new name for myself. At a 2014 home reunion, this was remembered very well, and we laughed about it.

We were listening to WROV, a rock and roll station which was broadcast from Roanoke. At the end of the song, the DJ announced that the song was a hit by Jackie DeShannon. And that song hit me like nothing I had ever felt before.

I started thinking, "Jackie DeShannon, Jackie DeShannon," and then lightning struck. I yelled out to my roommate, "I've got it!" And he said, "You got what?"

With huge excitement, I announced my new name audibly. "Jackie Dee Cunningham," I said, changing the singer's name to fit my desired last name.

I again ran to the director's office, very excitedly, and informed him that I had chosen my new name. And of course, he asked me what it was. I said with much pride and a lot of gusto, "Jackie Dee Cunningham," and he looked at me and said that it sounded like a girl's name. I was not deterred one bit and just told him that my mind was made up.

The name change legally took place in Roanoke County Court with the director and my stepfather, Haywood Cunningham, who actually agreed to adopt me for my name change. This would also begin a new relationship with my stepfather that continued to grow over the years until his death.

Most of my close friends and many acquaintances referred to me as "Jackie Dee" and still do to this day. I had a brand-new birth certificate with the name I picked on it. Remember, you can change things.

After all of this happened, I started the seventh grade at Broad Street Elementary School in Salem. I was fourteen years old and behind, even with catch-up preparation. I had started school at age seven and had failed the fifth grade. Well, at least I had a new name.

Chapter 5

(My Escape)

I no longer wanted to be in school. Reluctantly, the VBCH director permitted me to stop school at age fifteen and work in the print shop on campus. I had just started the eighth grade at Andrew Lewis High School in Salem.

Every teacher had told me that I was a bright child and could pass any grade as long as I took remedial courses in the summer before beginning the fall quarter. So, I was placed in eighth grade with the understanding that I would keep up in class, and stay for the duration, with peers in my age group.

The director had tried everything possible to help me get direction and to focus on something that would prepare me for the future. That included my going to see a psychiatrist, counselors, and having many tests done, both physical and psychological.

I had withdrawn into a deep dark area that had made it impossible for anyone to enter or to communicate with me. At this point in my life, I was a loner and as much as I tried to get beyond it, it was to no avail.

All the tests and reports were positive and indicated my capability of doing whatever I wanted. But therein was the problem. I wanted to do what I wanted and nothing else. It was surmised that I was a rebel and did not do well with authority.

The events that then took place propelled me into an entirely new environment yet to be experienced. I went to work in downtown Salem for the *Salem Times Register.*

My primary job was to prepare film negatives to be burned onto metal plates. These plates were used to print the newspaper. Other tasks were also assigned to me after completing this work.

My house parents at the time were not my biggest fans and had contempt for me that was impossible to not notice. And my contempt for them was just as bad, if not worse. I tried to avoid them at all costs.

One day, while I was working at the newspaper company, the offset press operator walked off the job and just quit. We had to gather all the material for the paper together to be driven to a newspaper company in Christiansburg in order to print the newspaper on time.

The paper was printed weekly, but we still had to make deadline. Of course, it never dawned on me or the manager to call the children's home to let them know I would not be back on campus at the normal time. This turned out to be a profoundly serious oversight.

When I arrived the next day at my cottage, my house parents attacked me with a viciousness that I had not experienced since living in Gladstone. My reaction was to defend myself until I could escape their hold on me and rid myself of the fist blows and open-handed face slaps. I will not sugar coat what I did next, and I don't believe they thought it was sugar coated either.

Drawing back my fist, I struck the man in his face and pushed his raging wife away as I walked out the door. I kept walking, since I knew this would be my last day as a child on the campus of the Virginia Baptist Children's Home.

(By the way, if anyone from the "Salem Times Register" is reading this, please send me my last paycheck. It's been fifty-nine years and I still have not received my last week's pay from you.)

I continued walking and contemplating where in this world I was going and questioning what I was going to do. This issue was very soon resolved by itself as it began a chilly rain. I was not dressed properly to be in a rainstorm and to top it off, I was nearly starving, having not eaten for almost a full day.

I had walked to downtown Roanoke and was seeking shelter from the rain. Glancing at a 1957 Chevrolet car parked on the street in front of a bar, I walked over towards it. Upon further inspection, I discovered the door was unlocked.

To make matters worse, the keys were in the ignition. To make it clear, I did not deem this to be a gift from God. Even I knew better.

Entering the vehicle, I observed very quickly that it was a straight shift, in the floor, with either three or four forward gears. There were three floor pedals to be operated, one of which was not familiar.

I had only driven an automatic previously but quickly became acclimated to this vehicle. I decided that maybe, just maybe, I could figure this out and drive the vehicle to escape the rain and get to my destination a lot faster.

All along, I knew that the only place I could go would be back to Gladstone, and I really did not know what the outcome would be. But it was soon revealed.

Not sure what gear I was in and not really caring, I drove down the highway. The Chevy had very loud mufflers, and each time I pressed the gas pedal, the sound coming from the twin pipes was overwhelming. I still love the sound of a '57 Chevy with dual exhaust.

I made it to Gladstone after driving on the wrong side of the highway for a bit. Not being used to four lanes of traffic with an island dividing them, I am quite sure the folks I almost hit will never forget this experience either.

I finally got my bearings and understanding of the highway system and made it to Gladstone. But I did tap another vehicle that was leaving Gladstone by passing it and coming back into my lane too quickly.

Upon arrival in Amherst, I paid my uncle Jessie a visit. Before heading out again, I gave him a carton of Lucky Strike cigarettes that I had found in the vehicle. My uncle appeared to be extremely impressed with the story told to him.

I did not mention several key issues. When we talk about it today, he always lets me know he didn't believe a word of what I said. I always ask why.

Soon after leaving my uncle's home and while driving to Gladstone, I felt ashamed and knew that I was running towards a home that did not exist for me. It was not going to serve me well to pretend any longer, and I made the decision to drive to Lovingston instead. I would turn myself in at the sheriff's department and deal with the consequences of the terrible mistake I had made. I was very scared and dreaded what I knew had to be done.

Upon arrival in the town of Lovingston, I spotted a lady walking down the street and asked her where the sheriff's office was located. She responded with, "Is there anything wrong, young man?" I then told her I had just stolen the car I was driving, and without hesitation, she gave me proper directions to the sheriff's office, looking very displeased as she did so.

After arriving at the sheriff's office and parking the car, I entered the office to find a dispatcher and Virginia state police trooper sitting and talking in the front room. After introducing myself and informing both officers of the deed that had taken place the prior evening, the deputy stated that they had been looking for the vehicle as well as its driver.

At this point, the deputy articulated that he was going to place me in a cell until I could be transported back to Salem. Now at this time, a most unusual event took place. The state trooper rose from his chair and informed the deputy that no such thing was going to happen. He, in fact, was going to take me to his home and have his wife fix a Sunday meal that would be enjoyed by all. The trooper lived in Lovingston.

Before this was to take place, the trooper had to obtain permission from the local judge. This meant going to a church on Route 29, where the judge was attending morning service, and there, getting his permission. It all fell into place.

We had a great meal, and afterwards, the trooper transported me almost into Bedford. He released me to a waiting policeman for the ride to a detention center.

(Years later, after locating this man on April 6, 2014, I was invited to his home and had the chance to say thank you in person for his being so kind to a troubled sixteen-

year-old boy, so long ago. The trooper was eighty-three years old at the time of our meeting again in 2014.)

By the way, I have always been partial to a 1957 Chevrolet Bel Air. I have never owned one but have definitely driven one!

Chapter 6

("Use of an unauthorized vehicle" Consequences)

A United States Marine recruiter once taught me that when communicating, certain terms and phrases sound better to people who sit in judgment of mistakes, particularly those made in youth. I somewhat agreed but still tend to use forthright language.

I was transported to the county sheriff in Bedford by the Nelson County assigned Virginia state trooper, to whom I remained grateful. I was then soon taken to the Roanoke Valley Juvenile Detention Center, on the outskirts of the city, to await a court appearance for "stealing the car." These are my words. Naturally, I've since learned it is best to drive one's own car.

As protocol dictates, a Roanoke city police officer drove the police car, escorting me to Roanoke. I missed the front seat view since I was sitting in the back seat. I thought about requesting the shotgun seat, but because the officer and I were getting along so well, I decided against it.

I was assigned a private, secure room within the detention center. My impression was this would be more than a typical overnight stay with only simple permission needed to leave. Sharp barbed wire, perfectly aligned, sat atop the high fences surrounding the complex. All gates were locked.

The staff monitored our every move. But we were allowed mail and visitors. The staff was genuinely nice to all the young children who were detained at the facility, and we had good, well-prepared meals, warm baths, and medical attention as needed.

I settled in and was pleased to learn that both females and males were present with the opportunity to engage in conversation from time to time. With total respect for my audience, events that would be deemed a bit risqué will not be interjected here.

There was plenty of time to adjust one's thinking and reevaluate one's goals in such a setting. My first thought was to become untroubled and avoid the appearance of needing discipline.

A caseworker had been assigned to me that would visit me and explain my predicament. I was pretty much aware of my plight, and it was not looking good, but I entertained his suggestions and knew instantly that my survival would depend on me.

It would be a month or so before I would be escorted to the Roanoke County Juvenile and Domestic Relations District Court. Finally, the day arrived. A judge would make a decision that would determine my future. I was nervous.

I was picked up by a Roanoke County deputy and driven to the courthouse early in the morning. As I entered the courtroom, unshackled and without handcuffs, I took note of all present and waited for the proceedings to begin.

One of the first things I noticed was my mother and her husband, whom I did not expect to see and did not want to see. I had not seen my mother often since I had been taken from her earlier in my life, at age three, and seeing her in the courtroom was uncomfortable. My mother and her husband now had three children together in the time since she left my first stepfather, Haywood.

I will refrain from going into detail about why I went to live with my great-grandmother and great-aunt other than to say it was in my best interests. But naturally, all these thoughts culminated and greatly affected my attitude towards my mother.

First, the judge asked me to stand as he introduced the man who owned the vehicle I had stolen. He appeared to be a genuinely nice young man, and the judge told me that this young man was not going to press charges against me. I do not remember if I said thank you or not. I pray that I did.

I could quickly tell that the judge was well versed in my case and did not beat around the bush with his assessment of me and his remedy concerning my predicament. He began respectfully by informing me personally that there were three options that he had considered, but he was not sure about one of these. Well, I was listening carefully, and based on his obvious concern for me, I felt that he was going to show leniency in my case.

He first mentioned the dreaded word "Beaumont" as the last place that he thought I should be sent to, and I silently agreed. Beaumont had a lousy reputation that prevailed throughout the juvenile detention system. I was relieved that he thought it unwise to send me there.

The next choice was a facility in Natural Bridge Station called the Natural Bridge Forestry Camp. This one caught me off guard. I had never heard of it. But I would be allowed to go there if they had an opening.

And then came a complete shock. The judge looked at me directly, with compassion, and stated, "I don't believe that you are a bad boy, and I am willing to give you a chance to be happy and an opportunity to go back to where you came from in the custody of your mother."

After what I had been through thus far in my life, the idea of going to live with her and her criminal husband was out of the question. But I also knew that my mother would be devastated if I said no, and I knew that I would feel bad for her as well.

I listened as she began to cry and plead with me to come to her home to live with her. I tried not to look at her, since I feared I would cry out of pity for myself as well as for her.

I stole a glance at my mother and knew that what I was about to say would have a profound effect on her. It really hurt me to know how bad she was going to feel.

Today, as I write this, I have tears in my eyes. I didn't hate my mother. Instead, I felt compassion for her, and again, without going into detail, I knew that I could not possibly make her understand my decision.

I looked directly at the judge, and with all the strength I could muster, I said, "Judge, I do not wish to return to where I came from with my mother or anyone else at this time, and I feel like, if possible, I would like to go to the camp that you mentioned earlier."

He said, with an ever so slight nod of approval, "I'll do my best for you. Good luck, Son." And he was true to his word. He did do his best for me.

It would be another month before I was notified that my acceptance at the Natural Bridge Forestry Camp (Natural Bridge Juvenile Correctional Center) had been approved. My caseworker arrived the day after this notification to drive me to the camp.

I passionately believe God was with me that day and helped me see through the midst of uncertainty. I was given wisdom and strength enough to take the best chance I was ever going to have at this point in my life. The remainder of this story is only further proof to me.

Chapter 7

(Natural Bridge Juvenile Correctional Center (NBJCC))

Natural Bridge JCC is a former Corps Camp that was converted for youth by the Federal Bureau of Prisons. The property became available in 1963. Funding from the Governor's discretionary fund was used to lease and operate the facility until the next legislative session could appropriate funding. (Pullen, 2010)

In early 1964, the first staff and residents arrived. The facility was the first of the juvenile correctional centers to be racially integrated in 1965. The NBJCC was originally designed to house lower-security risk, older, more stable youth. Both the Department of Corrections and the Department of Juvenile Justice (DJJ) operated the facility in this manner. (Pullen, 2010)

This facility was under a different name when Charles Manson spent a few months there. There is history of his stay found in articles, easily searchable, describing his behavior while there. These events were so profoundly disgusting that I will not entertain them in this book.

My caseworker and I were introduced to the superintendent of the facility. I was not particularly impressed with this superintendent from our initial introduction. Little did I know he would have so much authority and input to my stay and departure from the facility.

As I was being processed into NBJCC, little was said between a staff member and me. But my mind was on full alert as I realized that this was indeed going to be a unique experience.

After I received my very own set of regulation khaki clothes, I continued to assess my new environment. About twenty other young men and I were assigned to the first platoon where all new arrivals were placed.

After several days of working in the woods cutting trees and clearing brush from roadways, I settled in with the routine and relaxed a bit. We cleared the parking area at Cave Mountain Lake and were also assigned to work with the George Washington National Park Service.

I had not made friends with anybody, in particular, and really had no desire to do so. I just wanted to understand what this camp was all about and to try and understand my barracks mates. There were certainly a wide variety of personalities and a huge variety of heights and weights.

There were pack leaders and pack followers with neither group having any appeal to me. But I did notice one individual who was adaptable to both groups and who was moving around at his leisure without rejection from anyone. It appeared he was not large in stature, not assertive, and not necessarily concerned. I studied this young man, Rick, who would later become an incredibly good friend.

It dawned on me, after a short period of time, that Rick was highly intelligent, and he did not need to be assertive. I could tell that if required, he could hold his own in a conflict.

Needless to say, Rick and I became a team instantly, since there was an unspoken mutual understanding that this was not our desired world but surviving it would be paramount. Neither of us smoked or cursed much and usually did not enjoy the playing banter that naturally took place.

Rick and I read books, played cards, and went on our work details without complaint. Little did we realize that the NBJCC staff had being paying special attention to us.

They approached Rick and me to see if we would be interested in collaborating with a staff woman in starting a weekly camp newspaper. Not only would we get fewer assignments on work details, but we would be given a room in the gymnasium to design and publish *The Forester*, a name for the paper our lady mentor thought appropriate. We readily concurred since we wanted to start off on the right note.

We were extremely excited, and we loved our new project, and we adored this staff member who raised the question of whom we thought should be named the editor of the paper. I've always been really careful not to overstep my "fifth-grade" education level, and I didn't think my education level was up to the standard for that job title. So, I quickly claimed the title "assistant editor" of *The Forester,* and we moved on, with all in attendance agreeing.

I had not been at the camp long before I was informed that my great-aunt had died. She was the same great-aunt, along with my great-grandmother, who rescued me from my mother and abusive stepfather, when I was three years old.

The camp superintendent was well aware of my affection for this relative since he and I had discussed the subject just prior to her death. The decision was made that

I would not be able to attend the funeral, and I was terribly upset. But life as such went on.

Rick and I worked hard at everything we did, and a few months later, I was approached again and was informed that I would become a trustee. This meant that I would not be under the watchful eye of staff and would be given the freedom to move about pretty much as I needed or desired. This privilege also required that I be placed in honor barracks with the ten or so other trustees.

Just when I began to think that it couldn't get any better, I was called to the office to see the superintendent, who then talked to me about my childhood history again and about my future plans. He informed me that since I didn't have a home like most of the other kids, I would likely be required to stay at this facility until I was of age to be on my own.

But the great news was that I was going to be assigned the job of maintaining the grounds, which consisted of several acres of grass. I would also be given the privilege of operating and maintaining the brand-new cub tractor and to do so with complete freedom. At my discretion, I could cut the grass when and as often as I deemed necessary.

I left his office with mixed emotions. To say the least, his statement concerning the time of my release really bothered me.

We had team sports and we always had enough people to provide two teams. We once had a test of individual strength and assessment skills such as determining distance, height, and so on. I was not the biggest, and in all likelihood, not the brightest, but I was very strong. And to some degree, I was able to think, which in this particular contest, allowed me to win.

I remember the disbelief among the bigger kids when it was announced that Jackie Cunningham had been determined to be the overall winner. I remained calm and felt good about myself when I went forward to receive the trophy. The thinking part had been instrumental in my victory.

In my ten-month or so stay, I did have some conflict with a few people and actually had fights on two different occasions. My strength and the element of surprise assured my victory. I was never really challenged again, but I would receive a threatening stare from time to time.

The worst fight I engaged in occurred one evening after we had been driven, in our camp bus, to a local outdoor drive-in theater to see *Your Cheatin' Heart.* This movie was the Hank Williams story released in 1965 in the Buena Vista area. It was during the movie that a few of our fellow inmates began to laugh and make fun of the music and, of course, Hank Williams.

I asked them to stop so the ones who liked the movie could enjoy it. The camp supervisors did nothing to stop the disturbance. So, I told the troublemakers to stop again, this time receiving a very rude comment in return.

Finally, the movie was over, and as soon as we were returned to the camp and went to our designated buildings, I approached one of the troublemakers and addressed him in a fashion he did not like. He in turn slapped me in the face. That was not a wise move on his part.

This individual was much taller than me and probably stronger than I was, but I leaped up and grabbed him around his neck and forced his head down onto a steam steel radiator and began to pound his head against it. The only thing that allowed me to do so was the element of surprise.

He was bleeding and hurt and unable to get loose from my grip until a staff member pulled me off him. As we were taken outside the building and talked to, the guard asked if we would like to finish the fight with boxing gloves in the gymnasium. I agreed to the idea, but I really did not mean it because I knew this arrogant bastard would prevail in a supervised fight.

Thankfully, the staff made the decision not to let the fight take place. I never had any more trouble with this individual or his friends.

My girlfriend from the Virginia Baptist Children's Home came to see me along with her mother, who was visiting Brenda in Salem. Brenda had asked her mother to drive her to see me, and she did. I was happy to see her and disappointed that she had to come to this location, but her traveling this far meant a lot to me.

Things were going very well, but I realized that this situation was not going to benefit me overall, not regarding the future. Being a trustee in a juvenile correctional center was not preparing me for any potential employment opportunities that I knew of.

It was not long before I started to work on a plan to be released from state control, ahead of my projected release date. This was a huge gamble. But I was willing to gamble at this point.

Chapter 8

(Leaving Virginia)

After I had been at the NBJCC for several months, I kept thinking about a conversation I had earlier with the superintendent concerning my release. I devised a plan that I knew would work, if carefully orchestrated, and I weighed what actions would be taken if it didn't work. I was somewhat concerned about the latter for sure.

As a trustee, I was able to send a letter to a former houseparent at the Virginia Baptist Children's Home without it being read by the NBJCC staff before mailing. In the letter, I requested that Ms. Hayes contact a Marine Corps recruiter in Salem or Roanoke and ask him to visit me at the Natural Bridge Juvenile Correctional Center to discuss my joining the Marine Corps.

I had seen and heard the news about the escalating conflict in Vietnam and surmised that I could at least injure two birds with one stone. First, I would be released before my projected release period, making me incredibly happy. Second, the Marine recruiter would also be happy that he would have one less person to concern himself with, regarding his quota.

Well, I took stock of my present situation at the NBJCC, or rather, the Natural Bridge Forestry Camp, as it was called in 1964, when I arrived there. I thought about what I was giving up, and I determined that it was nothing compared to the freedom I would have in the Marine Corps. I put all my achievements, such as being made the assistant editor of the camp newspaper, being a trustee, having a cub tractor, and being team captain together, along with being the reigning winner of a recent superlative contest. All that just didn't seem so special anymore. Also,

I was getting tired of the same daily routine with every day being mostly predictable.

(To say that I was naive about all the freedom I would have in the Marine Corps was understated. Once I was given the chance to be a Marine, I realized I would have to be a little more precise in my future assessments, for sure, since my allowed freedom for the first few months was absolutely appalling. But I survived in good form.)

A few weeks passed, and again, I was beckoned to the superintendent's office. Once I approached the building, I observed a green military vehicle with the Marine Corps seal on the door, and I knew it was game time. I had to win this one. As I entered the office, I could feel the tension, and my dear superintendent was not smiling. This was not a good sign.

He was a rather huge man standing at least six feet two inches tall. Earlier in my stay at the camp, I had witnessed him discipline a fellow camper. I was scared, to put it mildly.

The first words spoken between the superintendent, myself, and the Marine recruiter were offered by my now very agitated former friend, the superintendent, when he loudly yelled at me, "Who in the living hell do you think you are to have a Marine recruiter come to my office under the impression that you are joining the Marine Corps?!"

And to expound upon just how serious the climate was in this office, let me share my thoughts for a second. If it were not for the presence of this sharply attired Marine wearing dress blues, I would most likely have been in a mild to severe coma after I had been struck in the face and fallen to the floor.

The rage continued as I was again introduced to the center's chain of command and proper procedure. Then silence took place, and I could hear my heart beating. I could undoubtedly see that the superintendent's heart was pounding too, due to the somewhat swollen jugular veins in his neck and his heavy and fast paced breathing.

I began to think that my first plan was not working. Then I was given an unexpected opportunity to speak and explain myself. Needless to say, the Marine recruiter was eager to hear my comments as I noticed that he had been very attentive. I had stolen a glance in his direction out of embarrassment as much as anything else.

Remembering the Roanoke judge's assessment of me helped here. "Mr. Bishop," I started, as I fought with everything in me to not cry and to stay calm and bypass the need to stutter. While uncontrollably shaking, I stated, "I am not a bad child. I have behaved myself while here, and I do not want to leave here unprepared and untrained to get a job when I am released. I honestly think I deserve a chance to improve my life and to accomplish something in the future. I don't belong here, and I don't want to be here any longer. And honestly, I don't believe it's fair that I am."

I was pleased, and then I cried at this point. I didn't care since I had no choice but to do so.

The Marine recruiter was the first to speak and to offer his sentiments. "Jackie, the first step to your entering the Marines is that you become seventeen years old. You are now sixteen." I had vaguely wondered about that issue.

He continued by saying, "We have to change a few wording issues, such as you did not steal a vehicle, but rather you had unauthorized use of a motor vehicle and instead of saying that your education level is the fifth grade, we are going to say now that it is the seventh-grade level." I was amazed at how quickly this meeting had changed direction.

The recruiter went on to say that after I turned seventeen in July, he personally would pick me up and take me to Roanoke to be mentally and physically evaluated for induction into the United States Marine Corps. At the end of this meeting, Mr. Bishop consented to the recruiter's plan.

I was so relieved and appreciative. This was spring of 1965. It was October of 1965 before the recruiter arrived at the camp again to take me to Roanoke, but I never questioned the delay.

Mr. Bishop never spoke with me concerning this meeting, and I really am not sure whether he was impressed with my performance or not. It mattered to me, but I didn't complain and made the best of the chance to leave. In the meantime, I stayed occupied with work as best I could.

Having had a visit from my girlfriend earlier, I knew what was best for her as well as myself. I wrote to tell her that I wanted to break up.

It was vital that I focus on becoming a Marine and being released from this facility. I did not want to be distracted. In fact, I never even mentioned to Brenda what my plans were.

Brenda took it extremely hard, and this bothered me greatly. Throughout the years, she never let me forget how much I had hurt her feelings. I apologized several times.

(I have been with my present wife, Judy, to the Virginia eastern shore several times to visit Brenda, and we always sent her a gift each Christmas and on her birthday.)

Parris Island, South Carolina, and preparing for the move there, began to be my focus. I was ready for a new challenge.

Early that fall morning, before departing to Roanoke for testing, I was awakened by a staff member and given my civilian clothes that I had traded in for the state issued khaki clothes that we all wore at the camp. I was then taken to the camp parking lot where the Marine recruiter was waiting. He then drove me to Roanoke.

There was no doubt of my passing the mental and physical exams based on how several bits of information concerning me had already been altered during my initial introduction to the recruiter in early 1965. My entrance into the Marine Corps required a waiver and I was well aware of the procedure.

These efforts, by both the NBJCC and the recruiter, made me appreciative, and I understood clearly that enlisting in the Marine Corps was my decision and mine alone. I held no malice towards anyone for my certain presence in Vietnam.

This was my plan, since it was my ticket out of the Virginia correctional system and a chance for freedom before I was too institutionalized to be a productive adult. As a child, I had experience. I had observed men who had been in prison and knew that they did not represent the kind of person I wanted to be.

After a few hours at the recruitment station, the fast-paced exams and tests were given. I was then again taken to the NBJCC camp to await transportation by the Marine recruiter to Richmond. There, I would be sworn into the Marine Corps and then transported to Beaufort, South Carolina.

The recruits would ride a bus to Parris Island to begin eight weeks of training. It was during the 60s that Marine boot camp stay had been reduced from twelve weeks to eight weeks to keep a steady flow of replacements for Vietnam.

Early on the morning of October 29, 1965, I again was awakened by staff at NBJCC. I put on my own civilian clothes to meet the Marine recruiter in the camp parking lot for the trip to Richmond and to finally say good-bye to the Natural Bridge Juvenile Correctional Center.

I had been incarcerated in the state system for over a year and will have to say without reservation or hesitation that this facility was operated by very caring, decent men and women who tried to help and direct young troubled boys to a more productive life. The work was hard, but not harmful. The food was good, and we were allowed the freedoms we deserved, and we were treated with utmost respect.

Punishment could be rough and quick if you decided you didn't want to follow the rules. If any boy became uncooperative or unruly, there was always a chance that person would be transferred to a stricter facility within the system.

It was also possible for a runaway to be physically beaten in front of others to set an example. It appeared to work as I only witnessed one such beating and knew of only one escape attempt, at this camp.

It is true that I had made several escape attempts while in Salem. But that behavior was absolutely not me, not anymore. I had become allergic to pain and public humiliation.

The trip to Richmond was uneventful as the recruiter would occasionally drive to a couple of predestined addresses to pick up recruits for the swearing in. Then came the train ride to Beaufort for the eventual bus ride to the wonderful and exciting world of Marine Corps training.

Chapter 9

(My Stepfather)

At this point in the writing of my story, I feel the need to expound upon a few things regarding my stepfather. Haywood Cunningham was my stepfather and my second cousin. His first cousin was my biological father.

Both men had been friends ever since they had known each other and often spent time together. They grew up doing many things together, including being present the night of my conception.

My mother needed Haywood because he provided the glimmer of security she needed, since she was dirt poor. Haywood never intended to marry my mother. He was just having fun.

But because he was always around my mother, he was threatened with being taken to court. So, he married her. Older folks know the term "shotgun wedding."

Haywood, despite what I've written about him, became my friend and came to my aid and rescue on many occasions later in life. Unbelievably, I eventually ended up viewing him as my only father. And yes, growing up, he was the only father I knew or had.

Maybe his change in attitude towards me was due to guilt or compassion or some combination. Regardless, I was very appreciative.

I never felt the desire to win his affection, such as one would in the Stockholm syndrome application. In fact, I avoided him as much as possible, wandering around the neighborhood and staying with different people when invited, and at the same time, becoming a rebel of sorts.

I remember coming back to the house where my siblings were one day, and he told me that I smelled like a wet dog. I had slept with folks the night before that had a dog. I also slept outside in borrowed tents or wherever I could to be away. It was degrading, and I felt it.

Haywood would though, on occasion, treat me very well and even bought me a used bicycle. I rode that bicycle every day as far as I could, stopping at country gardens along the way to eat tomatoes, cucumbers, and watermelons when available.

As time went on, the decision was made by the few responsible people in my weird world to place us in a children's home. Yes, he changed very gradually over a period of years.

The situation would become much better for me, as time went by, particularly as I myself was developing and accepting increasingly more of life's responsibilities. And he knew that.

Yet I did not confide in him regarding my plans for the Marine Corps. In fact, the only people that knew, besides me, were the recruiter and the camp staff. I had tunnel vision and wanted no distractions.

Chapter 10

(Semper Fi)

It was a challenge to open the possibility of joining the Marines, but it came to fruition. I entered through the gates of Parris Island on a fifty-six-capacity greyhound bus, fully loaded with recruits.

The training period was about to begin and would bring some recruits to their physical and psychological limitations. It was clear from the onset that the next few months would be as close to a nightmare as some could imagine. Some would remember it as hell.

The only things on Parris Island that bothered me were the sand fleas and the gas chamber (tear gas training). I did not mind the overall training and had a lot of respect for our drill instructors, who were in a class all their own.

Their interpretation of Dale Carnegie's book *How to Win Friends and Influence People* was slightly different from mine. But their approach did work.

I was seventeen and not very apprehensive. I was fascinated with the extreme reactions that some of the recruits were displaying to the shouting and screaming of the drill instructors, who were not in the least bit interested in winning friends.

With readers knowing my past, I feel no need to revisit each place with you. But I will add that having been a new kid on the block in several different, challenging environments, I was not in shock at Parris Island.

Maybe this was a disadvantage. I must admit it prevented me from taking the training as seriously as I should have.

I was in top-notch physical condition, and at this point in my life, there was not much that I had not seen or heard. I may have been a little damaged, but I was a long way from being broken, as you will understand as I continue this story.

Soon after my platoon was issued clothing and training gear, intense and severe training began. I'll not mention all the training but will focus instead on different events and behaviors I witnessed or was involved in.

I was not homesick. I had never been in an actual home situation in my life at this point, and I felt terrible for the recruits who were missing their homes and families.

Early into our routine, after standing at attention for a prolonged period, a recruit stepped out of line and shouted at the top of his voice, "Sir, I can't take this anymore, and I want to go home." Our senior drill instructor slowly walked down the squad bay and then stopped in front of the unhappy recruit and said to him, "That ain't gonna happen, Shit Bird," and the recruit responded with, "Sir, yes Sir!!" while stepping back into line.

Well, I must be honest. I could not control myself. I started laughing uncontrollably, even when the DI gave me his full attention. The DI ordered me to do jumping jacks for the next thirty minutes, and then I finally decided to stop laughing.

My laughing upset my instructors, and finally, my senior DI had a heart-to-heart talk with me after he hit me in the head with a rifle, telling me that my laughing days had better be over. And they were.

I was not being disrespectful when I laughed. I have a sense of humor. And even Parris Island did not change that part of my personality.

But I had come too far to let humor, which alleviated the stress of situations beyond my control, become a hindrance to me. So, I became serious. There were many more incidents that I wanted to laugh at, but I didn't.

The training was hard, even for me at times. And time passed very quickly.

I didn't write very much and didn't receive any mail. I was okay with that.

After finishing at Parris Island, North Carolina would be my next stop for further training. They separated me from my training unit because of my age. I was too young to be sent to Vietnam while still just seventeen.

During my first break, I traveled back to Gladstone to visit Haywood and his brother, Milton Cunningham, and stayed with them during this time. There is much to say about these two extraordinary men.

While on leave, I met a future wife who was visiting next-door neighbors of Haywood and Milton. We immediately started spending time together, and I knew that I would continue to see her whenever I could.

During the initial courtship, Milton offered me one hundred dollars cash to get on the bus and return to North Carolina if I would end the romance. In 1965, one hundred dollars was worth a lot more than today.

I understood the reasoning, but I said no. And after all the years, I would still say no. Money does not rule me.

The girl was from the Bent Creek area of Gladstone and had two children. She was also seventeen. She would be the first of my five marriages, all of course occurring at different times.

I mention my first marriage because so much happened during this period and afterwards. One huge event (Hurricane Camille) that was in the news eventually ended up described in a book titled *Torn Land*, written by Paige Shoaf Simpson and Jerry H. Simpson, and released in 1970.

(I worked in 1972 for J.P. Bell Company, the publisher of that book. Their location was on Kemper Street in Lynchburg.)

So, I returned to North Carolina without the hundred dollars offered earlier to learn that I was going to Quantico, Virginia, to work in support of the Officer Candidates School, again, because of my age. Arriving at Quantico just a few months after joining the Marine Corps was surprising but welcomed because I was closer to Gladstone.

Now, as always, something happened that was unexpected. After I had finished my evening meal and was on the way back to my barracks, I was stopped by a sergeant major that I had never seen before. Right off the cuff, he asked if I would like to be a military policeman.

I was stunned, and I looked him in the eye and asked him a question: "Sir, do you know who I am?"

The thought of being a military policeman was exciting, but I did not want to lose this privilege when he found out that I had just spent a year in two different juvenile detention centers. He did not smile when he said, "The Marine Corps knows who you are, and because you received a military waiver so you could join, it means you can do anything the Marine Corps wants you to do."

"Sir, where will I be stationed, and when do I leave?" I asked.

"The United States Naval Academy in Annapolis, Maryland, and you leave tomorrow," was his response.

Unbelievable. It would be hard to explain just how many times things like this have happened to me.

I honestly believe I have a guardian angel. I always have.

2   *Age 9*

1   *Jackie, 1951, age 3*

3   *The old smokehouse we first lived in*

4   *Age 13, my sister Virginia and me*

5   *Age 15, visiting Gladstone from children's home*

6   Age 14, visiting Lawrenceville, VA, foster home

7   *Age 15*

8   *Age 16*

9   *Age 17, Parris Island, SC*

10   *1966, military policeman, Annapolis, Maryland*

12   Vietnam, 1967, age 19   *13   Vietnam, 1968, age 20*

14   Vietnam, age 19

15   *1984, Vietnam Veterans Memorial wall, Washington, DC*

16 *Portrait of Judy and me by an
artist friend*

17 *Marine Corps League chaplain*

18   *1973, Rainbo Bakery, Lynchburg, VA*

19   *1976, Rainbo Bakery, Greenville, SC, crew*

Rainbo, Greenville

21   *Training in Dallas, TX, 1977*

76th Session Supervisor Seminar, Apr. 18, 1977, Dallas, Texas

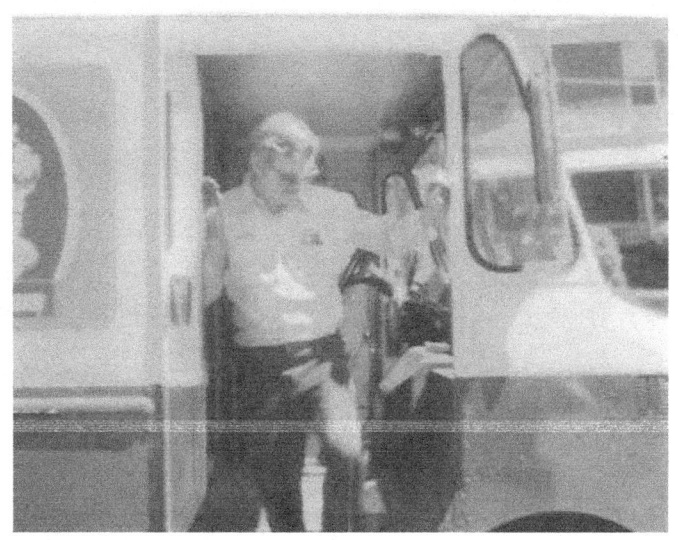

22　　　　　*1980s, working at Flowers Bakery*

23

24

1989, Miami, working for state of Florida

25   *1990, Lima, Peru*

26   *1991, Miami, having fun with some friends*

27   *1992, driving a tractor trailer*

28   *Judy and me, 1992*

29   *Wedding day, 1998*

30 Wedding day, Feb. 6, 1998

31

32   *Judy, myself, and our kids*

33

34

35   *2014, Lynchburg*

36   *2019, Hotel Roanoke*

37   *Judy, 1947, Allentown, PA*

38   *Modeling in Allentown, 1960*

40   *Whitehall High School, 1961*

39   *Judy, 1961*

41   *Tulum, Mexico, 1984*

42   Malcolm, 1970

43   March 2020

44   On a visit to Virginia Baptist Children's Home

45   *Malcolm*

46   *My best friend*

47   *My mother*

48   *My mother and her second family*

49   My mother (front left), her parents and siblings

50 Holding photo of second spouse

JACKIE CUNNINGHAM
MAMA MITCHELL

51

In Loving Memory of . . .

Mamie Tyree Mitchell

Born . . . . October 5, 1929
Gladstone, Virginia

Died . . . . February 22, 2006
Lynchburg, Virginia

Graveside Service
Sunday, February 26, 2006
2:00 p.m.
Evans Family Cemetery
conducted by the Rev. Ronnie L. Freeman

52

MAMIE FRANCES TYREE
CUNNINGHAM MITCHELL

OCT. 5.
1929

FEB. 22.
2006

53

54 Sylvia and me, 1967, Gladstone

55   In Amherst, 1966

56   Sylvia, 1966

*57   Sylvia's brother, myself, and her
sister at Sylvia's gravesite, 2016*

58

59   *Milton and Haywood Cunningham*

60   *Haywood and Milton, 1930*

61   My adoptive dad and uncle

62

63   Robert Wills, my biological
father

64   In the Navy

65   Robert, standing on right

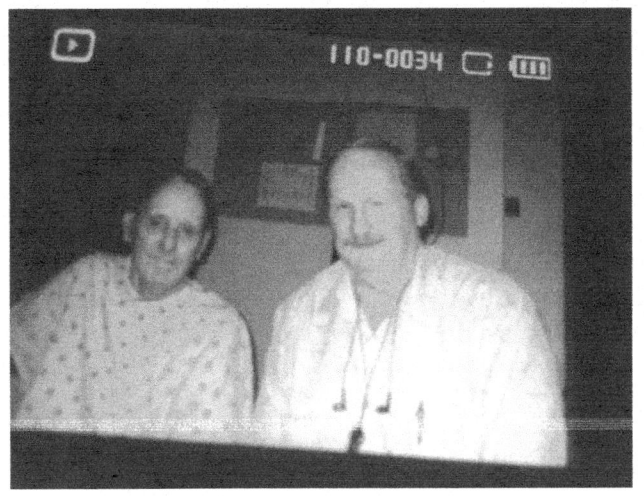

66   Visiting Robert in a nursing home

67

68   Younger days in the Navy

Ms. Hayes was my housemother at VBCH and a special friend who went above and beyond to help me attain developmental goals.

69

70   *The Virginia Baptist Children's Home dining hall*

The milk barn

71   *The milk barn where we milked cows*

Baptist Orphanage,
Salem Va.

salemorphanage.jpg
This is from a 1915 postcard.

72   *The administration building*

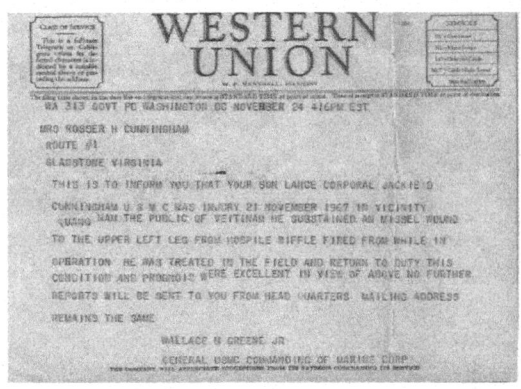

73

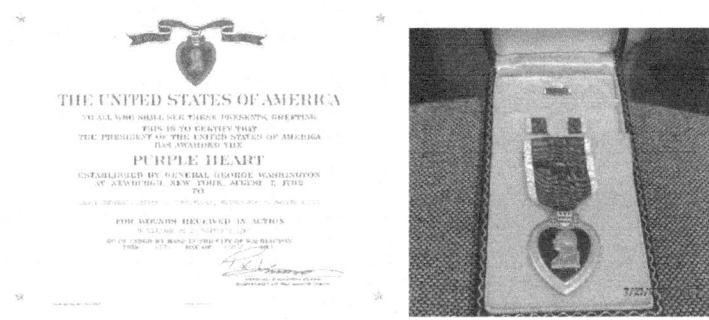

74   75

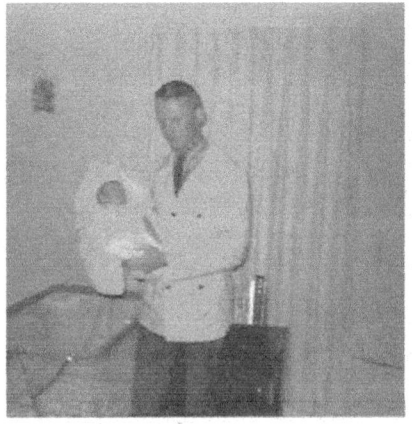

76   My daughter, Becky, 1972

77

78

79

80   Disney World, 1976

81

82

83   Great-Grandparents

84   Great-Aunt Peppie and Great-Grandmother Annie Megginson

85   Craig and Annie Megginson

86   Murphy Cunningham

87

88   The red Fiero Murphy gave me

89

90

91   *My mother and her children from her second marriage*

92   *My mother's first four children*

93   *My half-sister, Mary Ann*

94   *Judy, Mary Ann's husband Frankie, Mary Ann, and myself*

95   *Mary Ann, Frankie, myself, and Robbie, my other half-sister*

Chapter 11

(Annapolis)

Life as a military policeman (MP) was a very unexpected assignment for me, to say the least. It was not without trials and errors on my part. I have always been adventurous and being a military policeman did not hinder that part of me.

One night, on the midnight to eight a.m. shift, I was on roving patrol. This is when an MP is assigned a military police vehicle to patrol the assigned area of responsibility.

I became bored and decided to check out some areas within the base not on our normal route of travel. I detoured and decided to drive around the outer perimeter of the base golf course.

This was not a wise decision. It was only a few minutes into this uncharted path that I became mired in mud and got stuck. I tried and tried to spin my way out of the mud but could not free the truck.

I finally had to use my truck radio to inform the desk sergeant that I was stuck in the mud and needed help. When he asked me where my location was, I dreaded telling him that I was on the back side of the golf course.

After help arrived, it was determined that a Navy crane would be the only way to remove my truck and me from the deep muck. This was embarrassing, to say the least.

When finally, with the help of a Navy crane operator, I was able to return to our MP headquarters, a first sergeant summoned me to his office. While he was trying not to laugh, he told me that I would have to personally wash all our vehicles before I could go to bed. We had five vehicles. I was fortunate to have good and understanding superiors to work for, since I suspect punishment could have been worse.

-Our Mascot-

I was not only a military policeman at the United States Naval Academy. The Naval Support Activity base across the Severn River provided several different responsibilities, and one was guarding the Navy's mascot, a billy goat. We even kept a log of Billy and who actually entered his pen, which was located behind one of our sentry booths on the naval support side of the Severn.

Once, just before a Navy vs Army game, during the midnight to eight a.m. shift, two females approached the gate where Billy was. They somehow kept the Marine on duty so entertained and distracted that their two male accomplices were able to open the gate to Billy's pen and steal him.

After the Marine on duty later checked on the goat per standard procedure, he discovered that Billy was no longer in his pen, and he realized what had happened. The Marine had no choice but to report the missing goat and it did not turn out well for the Marine on duty that morning.

I never saw that Marine again and later heard that he was sent to a brig at another Marine base. This was very serious and embarrassing for our section of Marines. It could have been me on duty that morning and I am so thankful that I wasn't.

-The Navy Commander Who Knew Better-

There were areas on both sides of the river that were very restricted, and neither military nor civilian personnel were allowed to enter without escort or proper identification. The vehicle had to have proper bumper decals, and the driver had to have proper paperwork.

It was midday on a beautiful Sunday afternoon. I was in my usual happy mood enjoying my awesome historical surroundings as well as the constant parade of spectacularly beautiful young ladies. Their only mission in life was to capture the eye of a young midshipman for the possibility of a date and eventual marriage to the right man.

There were two directions that approaching vehicles could go when they reached my position. At a glance, I knew where they were allowed to enter or where they were not allowed to enter.

A small car with a Navy commander, a female front seat passenger, and a young girl and a young boy, in the back seat, approached my station. I saluted and asked for proper identification, since the car's bumper decal did not allow this vehicle to enter the area this commander wanted to enter.

The Navy commander was very rude and reluctant to be questioned by me when I asked for his credentials. He did not have the proper credentials and I offered a solution to his problem. I suggested that he present his case to my supervisors. I offered to make the phone call, which would allow him to speak with them.

When the commander realized that I was not going to permit him to enter the restricted area without authorization, he became very agitated and informed me that he was a naval officer with the rank of lieutenant colonel. He said if he wanted to enter, he would.

My mood had really changed, by this time, and I was very courteous when I said, "Sir, I am a lance corporal in the United States Marine Corps, and at this time, you will not enter the restricted area that you so desire." After a few seconds of what I surmised was a very unhappy moment for the commander, he placed the gear shift into reverse. He then turned around and left my area of responsibility, and I resumed my happy posture, smiling once again.

-Countdown-

With Ralph, my closest friend in Annapolis, recently getting married and being able to rent a house in town, I began to spend a lot of my off time with him and his wife. This was especially true when I did not have the money or time to travel to Virginia to see my girlfriend. But Sylvia did travel on occasion to Annapolis to visit with me.

I never really seriously thought about marrying Sylvia because I was seeing other women in Annapolis from time to time. Even though I did love Sylvia, I was aware of the fact that her own infidelities would resume. This proved to be true.

It seems that both Ralph and I were increasingly entertaining the idea of volunteering for Vietnam, mostly for the experience. And if we decided to stay in the Marine Corps, this would hopefully help in rank advancement. This was, at the time, our justification for doing such a thing. We had also asked to be sent to jump school and to be assigned to a recon platoon while in Vietnam, but due to a problem with my eyesight, that request was declined. Ralph withdrew his request.

At this time, marriage became a possibility for me, even though Sylvia and I never discussed it. If I were killed in Vietnam, my life insurance would benefit her and her two children. I did not mention to her that I was going to volunteer for Vietnam and thought we would marry before I mentioned it.

We continued to see each other and spend time together whenever we could and in August 1966, we talked about marriage and made plans for an October wedding, even though I knew the chances of our marriage lasting were very slim. Looking back, I firmly believe that I was attracted to my first wife because I saw in her the need for help my mother needed at her age. And this time, I had the resources and knowledge to help.

After our marriage, I spent another nine months in Annapolis. In July, Ralph and I volunteered to go to Vietnam. It was at this time that I confessed to Sylvia what I had done. It did not go over well.

For some reason, she thought I was trying to get away from her. I tried to explain, but she could not understand. I do believe she tried to be a good wife and was dedicated to our marriage for a while. But we were just eighteen and she was a very attractive girl.

In August 1967, my volunteering for Vietnam was approved. I would be given thirty days' leave to spend with Sylvia before meeting Ralph in Washington, DC to fly with him to California. From there, we would go through Vietnam indoctrination and other training at Camp Pendleton.

Most of the time, while home in Gladstone, we would spend our time in the house trailer that I had recently purchased for Sylvia. It was parked beside her parent's house. At other times I would go with her father to help at his small sawmill that was close to the house.

Sometimes this caused friction, but I enjoyed being around Sylvia's father and his crew and it gave me something to do. I was not a drinker but did on occasion have a drink at the end of the day. It was during this time that I deeply regretted volunteering to go to Vietnam, because I realized that I cared a lot more for Sylvia than I let myself believe in the beginning. But it was much too late to change the decision.

Soon, the time came to leave, and my stepfather, along with his girlfriend, picked Sylvia and me up for the journey to the Lynchburg, Virginia, airport. When we reached the airport, it became clear that this decision was not going to go well for me. And from what I could see from my window seat on the airplane, it was not going well for Sylvia either.

Haywood and his girlfriend were holding her as she collapsed on the tarmac gate, and that soon brought tears to my eyes as well. I turned my head away from my fellow passengers and the flight attendants to cry in private. But they all knew, since some were able to see what I was looking at.

When I arrived in Washington, DC and found Ralph, it was obvious that he had reservations about our decision to volunteer. He was leaving behind a wife and a newborn child.

It was a few days later, after we reached Camp Pendleton in California, that I realized what a real man Ralph was. It was after one of our training days was over, and we were allowed to have overnight liberty to go into town.

A friend that we had met approached us to see if maybe we wanted to go with him and a few other Marines into San Diego for drinks and to possibly pick up some female company. Before I had a chance to respond, Ralph spoke up and said, "No, I don't want to get drunk and spend any time with a girl that would take the place of my wife."

I was so glad I had not had the time to speak. I refused to go as well, and Ralph and I stayed on base and went to a movie.

Soon after this, Ralph and I received our orders, and we were assigned to different units. I was to fly to Okinawa for further transportation to Vietnam.

This was the last time I would see Ralph. He was later killed, and his wife wrote me a letter with that information.

Ralph was the best friend I had ever had, and as I write this book at the age of seventy-three, no one has ever come close to taking his place, with the exception of my friend that I was raised with in the children's home named Malcolm. Thank you, Ralph, for being the kind of man you were and for dedicating your life in service to our country.

Chapter 12

(Vietnam and the Return Home)

I arrived at Camp Pendleton in August 1967. A short time later, I went on to Okinawa.

Time from this point seemed like it slowed down, especially after arrival in Vietnam. I'll not share war stories other than to mention a few things that happened that were significant to me.

Soon after entering the country, during the first month, I was flown to the Danang hospital because of drinking contaminated water and having to be treated for more than my share of parasites. I spent about a week there. I don't advise anyone to drink from a rice paddy.

The next big thing that happened was I was shot in my left leg on November 21, 1967. That turned out to be minor, and I was able to remain in the field.

But I continued to be plagued by stomach problems. This meant being flown by helicopter to the USS Repose hospital ship in the South China Sea.

Next came the event that really hurt. I received a letter from my wife that was to be the beginning of the end of our marriage. To make a long story short, I was distraught. In between her lines, I realized another man was in the picture. I requested emergency leave and was, of course, denied.

When I was in California awaiting discharge papers from the US Marine Corps at Camp Pendelton, I went into town to a bar to order a drink. But, before the mixed drink arrived, a song by the Beatles called "Yesterday" began playing on the jukebox. I immediately played it again after it was over.

I identified with the song and knew this would not be the evening I had planned. I then paid for the drink and did not touch it. But instead, I got up and hailed a taxi to take me back to the base, since this was not a night that needed to be fogged by strong spirits.

I faced a sobering decision and needed something real that didn't come in a bottle. I prayed.

The only real option was to go back to Gladstone and talk to Haywood and Milton Cunningham about my situation. I had considered writing a letter in advance to address the issue but felt that face to face would be better. And they did know about Sylvia and me.

After flying into Lynchburg, I called a taxi to take me to Gladstone. The day was cold and snowy, and I arrived in the late afternoon, unannounced, with everything I owned in my seabag that had been issued back in boot camp.

I had wisely saved money while in Vietnam and had a few dollars in the bank. There was enough in my pocket to go to a motel if necessary.

Both men were sitting at the dinner table when I entered the house, and they greeted me and told me they were expecting me. We chatted for a bit, and then I decided to go for it.

I asked if I could move in until I could get my bearings. They agreed to the idea. There was not much to move.

The first important thing on my mind was to file for a divorce, and I went to see a lawyer in Amherst. My divorce was finalized quickly because of the circumstances that prevailed.

There was no real need to see my ex-wife, but I decided to visit her and her boyfriend, since I had left a few personal items with her before I left to go overseas. This was not a great idea.

The boyfriend was not a happy camper, and just after I had entered their house, he asked my ex-wife where her pistol was. This was a pistol that I had left with her for protection while I was gone. She refused to retrieve it.

My emotions were quite strong regarding this strange hostility that had surfaced. After determining that the items were no longer available, I excused myself.

Not so long after the incident happened, my ex-wife called me and wanted to talk. This was not a great idea either.

I agreed to meet her at a friend's house, and after an hour or so of talking, I told her that there was no future for us. As we were getting ready to go our separate ways, my friend informed me that the boyfriend had arrived.

I asked Sylvia to stay in the house, and I went outside to talk to her boyfriend. As I approached his car, he pointed the same pistol at me.

Walking up to him, I reached up and put my arm around his shoulder. He began to cry and then put the pistol down.

Asking him to stay in the car, I went back inside the house and asked my ex-wife to follow me. I opened the door for her and requested that she sit in the front seat with her boyfriend. Then I leaned over to the window and told both of them to stay away from me. This meant no letters, no phone calls, and no messages.

Sometime after that, I was in a car accident requiring me to be taken to Lynchburg General Hospital for a few days. Sylvia came to visit me there. That would be the last time I would ever see her alive.

I worked in Harrisonburg for an electric company out of Roanoke that put in control panels for electric substations. I only came back to Gladstone on the weekends.

On August 20, 1969, for some unknown reason, I decided to drive back to Gladstone. I was restless and just needed to take a ride. It's hard to explain because I never went home during the week.

Once I passed Waynesboro and headed towards Piney River and eventually to Route 29, I was stopped at the bottom of the mountain by a state trooper. I was told that if I wanted to drive to Gladstone, I would have to go to Richmond and enter from the east.

A catastrophic flood had taken place in Amherst and Nelson counties. This was the first I had heard this.

Upon arriving much later in the evening, I saw people standing around in Bent Creek looking at the James River, which was extremely high. Then I stopped and asked some friends to tell me what in the world was going on.

After learning that Norwood had been hit hard by Hurricane Camille, I asked if they knew anything about Sylvia. But I really didn't have to ask. I already knew.

A few days after the flood, bodies were found and continued to be found for some time to come. Sylvia was found high in a tree after the water receded. The tree was not far from where the house she was living in was washed off its foundation.

Her house had been carried down the river with extreme force. A man standing on the bridge that the house crashed into saw Sylvia on the porch of the house holding a child. Nobody knows for sure which child since she had three at the time. My understanding is she was also expecting another.

Even though Sylvia and I were divorced, it did not lessen my love for her in any way. I agreed with Sylvia's mother and father that I would be the one to go to Lovingston, where a lot of recovered bodies were being placed in body bags and stored in trailers to await possible identification by loved ones and family members.

I unzipped every bag that was available, bound and determined to find her. Some of the bodies were unidentifiable, but I kept looking.

After I found out that her remains had been taken to a funeral home in Dillwyn, I immediately drove there. When I arrived at the funeral home, I was denied my request to see what was left of Sylvia because she and I were divorced.

I asked the staff to call the sheriff's department. I was going to go into the holding area that contained Sylvia's remains, whether or not permission was granted.

At that point, I was allowed to view what was left of her. Even though her face was missing, I recognized the shorts she was wearing. I had seen her in them many times when we were married.

I had seen some terrible things in Vietnam but seeing someone that I had loved in this condition, with almost all of her flesh missing, was a different thing entirely. At least, I was satisfied that it was her, enabling some degree of closure.

Sylvia Gale Gunter Cunningham, Junior Burnley, and their children, perished in Hurricane Camille on August 19, 1969. Sylvia's and only one child's remains were found. She was just twenty years old. Many years later, I learned that Sylvia's grave did not have a marker of any kind, so I had a large one made.

(My wife Judy has encouraged me to write this part to come to terms with some reality of the missing parts that I seldom share regarding the past.)

When her burial took place at her sister's house, I was standing alone when a woman I knew approached me and took my hand. She softly asked me to come by her house once the funeral was over.

I wasn't sure if I should or not, but I was miserable and needed something or someone, so I went to her house. When I arrived, she opened the door and took my hand once again and led me to her bedroom. She hugged me while I was lying on her bed, crying.

I know what you may be thinking. That woman helped me that day and gave me the comfort I desperately needed. After that, every time I was near her home, I would stop and thank her for helping me on such a sad day. Sometimes, I would have no other conversation with her but to say, "Thank you." She would only respond with, "You are most welcome."

Even unto this day, I still remark, "You are most welcome," due to remembering the sincerity in that lady's voice. Her understanding and knowledge of what I was going through meant the world to me.

Chapter 13

(Freedom)

Returning to Gladstone was awkward with many uncertainties, to put it mildly. But the nearest thing to a home that I had ever known was the one Milton and Haywood provided.

I quickly became aware that I was now not in the structured environments I had been in for the last nine years. And that made me feel pretty insecure.

My childhood was rarely free of stress or pressure, and the result of that was going to surface in my subsequent behavior. After receiving my civilian driver's license and purchasing a vehicle, it was a wild ride for the next several years.

Living in Gladstone again was quite an experience. I didn't realize just how many people I was kin to or connected to for various reasons. I once dated a cousin that I liked a lot without knowing what close kin we were.

Once we broke up, she told me that the only reason I broke up with her was because she wasn't my sister. I still enjoy her humor after all these years.

I had never lived a normal childhood and was about to go "plumb crazy" at the age of twenty, trying to experience things I had missed or thought I had missed. Most things I did were not what any normal person would do at any age.

I was reckless and didn't work anywhere for long, just long enough to put gas in my car and take off again. Once, I ended up in North Carolina with a friend and ran out of money. We became so hungry that I drove to the town's police station and asked them to lock me up and feed me.

My friend agreed with my decision. The chief laughed and said he had a better idea. He called a local printing company that needed help and we were hired.

At the end of the first workday, I asked the supervisor for a pay advance so I could eat. We were given twenty dollars apiece.

We promptly purchased several hot dogs and then filled my car up with gas and drove to Nashville, Tennessee. Finally, I called Haywood, and he wired me money to enable me to drive back to Gladstone. I would continue this sort of nonsense for quite a while.

I was dating from time to time, and it wasn't too long before someone caught my eye in a town some distance from Gladstone. We went out from time to time, but nothing serious developed, and we both saw other people too.

Several months into our dating, her mother invited me to have dinner, and I was surprised to realize that the dinner was just for her daughter and me, with her mother waiting on us. "This is a bit odd," I thought, noticing a lit candle on the table.

As I was leaving after dinner, my date's brother came home, and I learned that he was a preacher. I could surmise from the initial meeting that he and I would not be doing any missionary work together.

I mentioned all this to Haywood and Milton because I was still living with them at the time. Well, this time they didn't offer me a bribe to leave town like before, but they strongly recommended that I seriously think about what was appearing to transpire.

I didn't go back to that town to date the girl anymore and about a month later, she called to tell me she was moving to Florida and that she was pregnant. I asked if she knew who the father was, and she said it was me.

Well, I was sure hoping it wasn't me, but nevertheless, I asked another favorite uncle to go with me to talk to the girl. Upon arrival, the preacher brother came outside of the house and walked to the car.

He told me not to get out of the car and to never come back. I explained the reason for my visit, and then he got really mad. My uncle suggested we leave, and we did.

I was never able to speak to the girl again, but many years later, I did some research and concluded that she never went to Florida. And even though she did have children, their birthdays did not coincide with the time period that we dated. She married someone else, and I am quite happy for her and even happier for myself.

I found work but was so unsettled that work would be temporary. I moved from job to job with ease and did not take anything seriously. I was becoming a child again only this time spending money and enjoying things that I had not experienced in childhood nor young adulthood.

In the next few years, I would be involved in eight car wrecks and would end up in the hospital because of two. In the most serious of the two, I was not driving.

Because of these careless and unpredictable ways, I was asked to leave the house I shared with Haywood and Milton. Haywood took me to Brockman Chevrolet in Amherst and bought me a 60s model Chevrolet Corvair, since I had recently wrecked my car. Then he paid my rent for a month at a local motel. It was time for me to make it on my own.

I knew all along that Gladstone was not going to be where I would stay very long. Even much later on, after I acquired seventy-eight acres of land and a house, I knew that location would bring back so many memories that would keep me from relaxing and enjoying life there.

There was resentment from family members, original property owners, and even people who were not in the family. Events and attitudes regarding my inheritance are mind boggling to this day.

It worked out though. My nature was to be restless and to search for something different, even at a young age. I was always inquisitive and enjoyed a challenge. There was always the desire to improve my life.

Most environments that I experienced from the age of eleven until the age of twenty were the direct result of my actions and planning. I was so fortunate to have good people assist me and come to my aid, repeatedly, offering guidance and making good things happen that I had no power on my own to do.

Being told what to do, when to eat, and what to wear in the children's home, the detention center, and the Marine Corps, in my opinion, had institutionalized me. But those institutions had given me the structure I so desperately needed, with the result being a disciplined and controlled way of life.

Suddenly finding myself, at age twenty, with none of those restraints and commands put me at a loss, in a manner of speaking. But I knew money was necessary to live, no matter what.

I was hired at the Lynchburg Foundry and moved to Washington Street in Lynchburg. After an injury at the foundry, I moved to Amherst and rented a room.

Then I worked for Burton Construction Company in Lynchburg. It was soon after this that I met a girl with whom I had a serious relationship.

We met at a local school dance, dating for a while, and then marrying in 1970. This marriage produced my only child, a daughter.

We rented and moved into a house just below Amherst High School. I had left the construction company and was now working for Amherst Publishing

Company. Then I went to J.P. Bell Company, another publisher located in Lynchburg.

I had met a man in Madison Heights, where we lived at that time, on the same street, and he asked me to leave my printing job and go into route sales. He was a sales supervisor from Hillsville, Virginia, and this man was a salesman that was as successful as any I've ever met in my life.

I was very reluctant to leave my job and explained to him that I was not a social person at all, with no confidence in my selling ability, but Moe would not give up. He invited me to go to a Martinsville car race with him. The idea was to give me a sales pitch to and from the race when he had me in the car, and I had to listen to him.

It worked. After returning to my job at J.P. Bell Company, I gave my notice and went to work for Rainbo Bakery in 1973. I was very unsure of myself, but I accepted the challenge, and to put it bluntly, the first year was a complete nightmare.

It was unbearable since I had no selling skills. It was hard for me to start conversations.

When meeting store managers for opportunities to increase my sales, I was not tactful at all. I just said what was on my mind.

I didn't give a hoot about baseball, basketball, or football. If I had a lady customer and she talked about crocheting, I didn't care about that either. I liked racing, boxing, reading, and music. But I never even talked with anyone about those things either.

It was just plain hard for me to start a conversation in the public domain. That would change.

My new friend was being transferred to Greenville, South Carolina. After he moved, he called and suggested that I also bring my family to Greenville to help Rainbo

Bakery out of Johnson City, Tennessee. We would start a new market in South Carolina.

I had already concluded that I was going to continue in sales. I was improving my selling ability and knew that this job was helping me grow in confidence. So, I was determined to stick with it. We arrived in South Carolina in 1974 and spent the next six years in Greenville and in Charlotte, North Carolina.

While in Greenville, during the first year, I was promoted to sales supervisor. With a good increase in my pay, Rainbo Bakery began to send me to sales seminars in Tennessee and also in Dallas, Texas.

Public speaking was a required class. This was not on my list of things I wanted to do in this lifetime or the next, and I considered not going to Dallas. But I did.

Before I left Greenville, the vice president of the bakery called me into his office and gave me a check for expenses. It was a fair amount for my week's stay in Dallas.

I thought little of it and assumed it was mine to keep and to spend as I wanted and pleased. This was not the case.

When I returned to my office after the week in Dallas, the vice president came in to ask how much money I had left over from what he had given me. I told him that I had nothing left and actually had spent some of my own money. He laughed and said, "Your next check will have a deduction on it."

He knew I misunderstood. I had to pay back what I spent on entertainment. I still tell that story every so often.

While in Dallas, after class, I went out to nightclubs in the evenings and danced the night away while having mixed drinks and excellent meals, in restaurants, with others in my class. It was awesome.

During the days, we had classes on different subjects. Finally, at the end of the week, each of us was expected to stand before a room full of our instructors and classmates and give a fifteen-minute talk on any subject we wanted. It was referred to as extemporaneous or off-the-cuff talking.

I chose doorknobs, and as I started, I just got carried away and was really enjoying myself making things up as I went. I haven't shut up since that day in 1976.

After returning to South Carolina and home, I was sent to Indianapolis, Indiana, for a week of working on a union strike. Talking became vital for learning about the city and where places of business were located. I had to talk to people and calm them down. They had not received bread needed to open their restaurants.

It was during the Indianapolis 500 that the union had chosen to go on strike so that it could have the biggest effect. Because so many people attended the race and the fast-food restaurants, bread was crucial to these businesses staying open.

One man ran to the vehicle I was driving and opened the back door, grabbing an arm full of packaged hamburger buns and throwing them on the floor of his restaurant. I said to myself, "What the heck?" and did the same thing.

I then asked where he wanted the rest. He calmed down, and together, we picked up the buns and placed them on the shelf.

Another stop was a little funnier than that. As I walked into an Orange Julius store, a lady screamed at me and asked, "Where in the hell have you been? I've been out of bread for a day!"

I couldn't help myself when I replied, "I don't know where in the hell I've been and don't know where in the hell I am now!" She started laughing and seemed more relaxed. I was too. The week ended up being an experience that I didn't want to go through again though.

It was not long afterwards that my second wife and I divorced. My second wife was an extraordinary lady that deserved to have met a better man than I was at the time. I take full responsibility. I was not happy, and the truth be told, I had not fully gotten over my first wife and was in mental turmoil. I simply was not happy, in general.

Rainbo Bakery wanted me to move to Anderson, South Carolina, roughly thirty miles from Greenville. I was told to hire six people to fill the bread routes that were operative within that area. I had known about this proposal from the grapevine before the vice president told me about it.

I spoke to my division about moving, and all of my salesmen wanted to work for me and agreed to drive from Greenville to Anderson each day. It really meant a lot to me that they were willing to do that.

Then, I informed the vice president that he and the sales manager would need to hire six people. My men were going with me. He was a little surprised, to say the least.

My salespeople and I were a close team and won the most selling contests that the bakery had. My sales figures were very consistent with the growth that was expected by upper management.

It was not long afterwards that I was asked to move once again, this time to Charlotte. Rainbo had purchased the old A&P Bakery there. We would be in a new market for Rainbo products.

My third and fourth wife were the same person. She was from South America. We met at work. Again, she was a great person, and I take full responsibility for the ending of both marriages to her. I was still carrying the same problems.

It was about the time of establishing new work in South Carolina that I began feeling very unusual and downright abnormal. My problems, personally and professionally, were about to get even more serious.

Chapter 14

(Back to Virginia)

I suspect that I would become disoriented because of the relentless panic attacks. Traveling in a car, I would become claustrophobic and would have to stop and exit the car.

Sometimes, I would lie on the shoulder of the road while hyperventilating and waiting to regain some sort of composure. It was somewhat embarrassing if I was with someone I didn't know very well.

The problem had gotten really bad. Once, while I was having breakfast in a restaurant, I happened to pick up a newspaper off the counter and saw the word "Vietnam." I immediately had an attack that caused me to leave the restaurant without finishing my breakfast. Eventually, it was tough for me to leave my house.

Strangely, I also became sick with the same ailments that plagued me in Vietnam and was given a service-connected disability identification card from a Veterans Administration hospital. The VA diagnosed me as having PTSD (Post Traumatic Stress Disorder).

After about a year in Charlotte, I requested a transfer back to my home state. I wanted to go back to route sales and no longer desired to be a supervisor. I knew the PTSD was getting worse by the day.

The president of Rainbo Bakery in Roanoke refused to let me go back to route sales and wanted me to stay in supervision. I did not tell anyone about my PTSD. Only the Veterans Administration and my wife knew.

I even talked to Flowers Bakery in Lynchburg since I knew the vice president at that location and asked if he would pay my moving expenses if I came to work for

Flowers. He and I had worked together while he was in Tennessee.

Larry told me if I agreed to come to Lynchburg as a supervisor, Flowers Bakery would pay the moving costs. I refused the offer.

Rainbo agreed to transfer me to Staunton, Virginia, but I had to stay in my present position. I agreed.

I moved to Middlebrook, next door to Staunton, and knew it would not be for long. It was to the point that I began to drink alcohol for relief from my symptoms.

One day, I purchased a guitar in Waynesboro, while working. I drove to Staunton and entered the Rainbo thrift store. Once inside, I began playing my guitar and singing "Fraulein." My singing and playing were terrible.

I thought nothing of it until the next day when the president of the bakery called and requested that I come to visit him in Roanoke. "Well," I thought, "at least I will end up in Lynchburg with Flowers." I was close enough to move without too much expense.

When I entered the president's office in Roanoke, it was quick. He said, "I am going to give you severance pay, and you are fired." I responded with, "Thank you, Sir," and thought to myself, "I've got to practice my playing and singing for sure."

Larry at Flowers hired me on the spot the next day. I moved to Martins Lane in Madison Heights.

I was given a sales route in downtown Lynchburg, and I loved it. But it did not take away my problems, and the PTSD continued to get much worse.

One of the most embarrassing moments happened one day when I was delivering bread and had a severe panic attack in a store on Old Forest Road, in Lynchburg, less than a mile from Lakeside drive. I was unable to drive my delivery truck.

I was on my knees when I asked a store employee to call the bakery to send someone to get me. There were no cell phones at the time.

The VA was giving me medicine and suggested that I come in for counseling in Salem. I'm not the type to want to talk or even listen to fellow veterans relay events that happened in Vietnam or elsewhere. I've only had these discussions with a handful of people.

I am sure I could have gotten a disability rating, but I chose not to. I just did not want to go through that procedure.

In the meantime, I came off of the route and just worked alone, doing what was needed for the bakery, until a miracle happened. The situation had gotten to the point where I could barely leave the house for work unless I was full of medication.

One morning, around 2:00 a.m., I was sleeping and was suddenly awakened by a warm feeling. What felt like a hand touched my forehead, and it just "went through my head." No words were spoken, and no sound was heard, but in my mind, I felt complete peace.

Whatever it was (and I believe it was God) communicated that I would no longer need the medicine to function. At first, I was sure it was a dream, but just before I turned to awaken my wife, it happened again. I said a thank you without speaking, and the warm, glowing feeling was gone as quickly as it came.

When it was time to go to work, I did not take my medication, but I took it with me, just in case. Throughout the day, I was expecting to need the medicine just to do my work, but that didn't happen. To this day, I still don't take those meds.

Rarely, I might have a nightmare and wake up sweaty, having dreamt about events in Vietnam, but not to the extent that I can't function, like it had been previously.

These rare occurrences usually pass without any problem.

I've shared this story over the years and enjoy telling it. I genuinely believe it was a miracle.

Time passed, and I went back to work in route sales until I left the bakery in 1987 for a short job stint at Belgium Tool and Die in Lynchburg. But I soon had another offer.

Chapter 15

(Miami)

I left Lynchburg and moved to Miami, Florida. A friend of mine worked at a detention center there, and he suggested that I apply for a job.

Upon entering the complex and asking where the personnel office was located, I noticed that this was indeed a busy place. I knocked on the door and was immediately invited in for an interview.

The first question asked was, "Were you military?" I answered that I was, and she then asked what branch. I told her the Marine Corps. The interview stopped, and she stood up and said, "Follow me."

I was taken to a classroom where several other new people were and was told that I was hired. I had not even filled out the application yet, but I did later.

After class was over, my uniforms were issued to me, and I was told to report the next day for more classroom training. Within the week, I was sent to the police pistol range to qualify with a pistol and shotgun. Then it was back to classroom training again.

Our job was to transport inmates from the courthouse to a classification center. From there, they would be sent to their final destination to serve their sentences.

It was hot and crowded in Miami. I made friends and worked with a lot of Spanish-speaking folks while employed there.

The population of the inmates being processed at any given time was about nine hundred. Most of the people were very well behaved, cooperative, and caused little trouble. This was rather familiar territory to me, and it was good to be in a position to go home at night and not have to stay detained as a client this time.

It was enjoyable talking to the inmates and learning a little about them. I was surprised to learn that we had several former police officers who had committed crimes and were going to be with the system for a while.

One reason for going to Florida was that my third wife and I had separated, and I was interested in possibly reconciling. Even though she was from South America, she had spent a lot of time in Miami growing up. While there, we decided to travel to South America so I could meet more of her family.

Lima, Peru, was an interesting place with lots to see and explore. My wife had an aunt who had been told that I was coming for a visit. She learned that I enjoyed cold beverages, and this lady went out and purchased a new refrigerator so I could enjoy those cold drinks. I tried to pay for the refrigerator, but she would not take any payment. I was really touched by her kindness.

While in Lima, I decided to visit the prison but was denied entrance. That was no surprise, but I tried.

I am adventurous and would sometimes walk along investigating things, and my friend, a Lima policeman, told me not to do that. The Shining Path, a Peruvian revolutionary organization that endorsed Maoism, was known to capture Americans and demand a ransom. They were afraid that could happen to me if I went places alone.

Leaving Lima, I had an unexpected surprise when I was apprehended at the airport while trying to get a close look at a Russian Aeroflot airplane. My mother-in-law was small, but she was a lion when she was mad. After I failed to return to the waiting area, she started looking for me and saw what had happened.

I'm not sure what she said to the police officer, but I know that I was released immediately with instructions to not go near any airplane other than the one that we were to board. We stopped in Quito, Ecuador, to pick up passengers and then went on to Panama for another stop before returning to Miami.

This time, a flight attendant stopped me from getting off the plane to explore. Due to that country's laws, I could be arrested. I was like The Flash as I made my way back to my seat.

After arriving back in Miami, I had already made my decision to return to Virginia. I told my wife that if she wanted to go with me, she was welcome, but the decision was up to her. Miami was too hot and too crowded for me.

I returned to Virginia alone and stayed with a friend that I had met in 1969 after returning from Vietnam. We had dated for a while.

It was never hard for me to find a job. Returning to a previous employer was not a problem, so I went back to Allen Morrison Sign Company in Lynchburg.

Eventually, I wanted to travel again and decided that seeing the USA in a Chevrolet was a great idea, but I would drive a tractor-trailer instead. I took a class to obtain my CDL license and went to work for Harris Trucking.

I traveled to Canada and thirty-two states in less than a year. And my wife did return to Virginia.

After she arrived, she insisted that I drive to see my roommate and officially declare to my roommate that I would not see her again. There was no need for me to do that, but I went ahead and made this declaration, to my roommate, in the presence of one of my wife's friends. My wife had sent her friend to witness what was said.

The declaration would be in vain, as my marriage eventually ended. This would be my fourth divorce. I was married to my third and fourth wife (same woman) a total of fifteen years, twelve the first time and three the second time. We used the same attorney, since we were still friends and did not want anything from each other in a settlement.

On one occasion, well after our divorce, she called me and said she wanted to talk. I foolishly agreed, and when we met, she asked me to sit in her car. I did. After I sat down and shut the car door, she started driving away from my parked car.

I told her to stop, but she wouldn't. It would take her several miles before I convinced her that she and I were really finished. She then returned me to my parked vehicle.

I drove away with the understanding that a break from her would be necessary to continue with life as I envisioned. We would discuss business and family matters but only cordially at best. I emphasized to her repeatedly that our lives would be independent of each other from this point forward.

Chapter 16

(Seeing the USA)

In 1992, driving around the country in an International diesel truck suited me very well. My wife had returned to Virginia, and our situation deteriorated, but the following story makes me smile.

I was in Ohio, near the city of Columbus, on a very cold December night around 3:00 a.m. Usually, at this time of morning, I would become very tired regardless of the time of year.

I was trucking along, listening to my favorite two country artists, Patsy Cline, and Ray Price, with occasional songs by Marty Robbins. I was driving a tad over the speed limit to reach my next destination before sunrise, thereby avoiding heavy traffic.

Glancing at my side view mirror, I was really not surprised to see flashing blue lights approaching my truck at a high rate of speed. Slowing down, I eased to the shoulder of I-270 and stopped. All of a sudden, an Ohio state trooper was at my door and was climbing up to my driver's window. He began pounding on my door and demanding that I roll the window down.

At this moment, I thought his behavior to be completely unnecessary, overly aggressive, and uncalled for, to put it mildly. After my window came down, he informed me that I was speeding and had a trailer light out. As mentioned before, it was very cold, so he ordered in a very unpleasant tone for me to bring all identification and my driver's logbook to his vehicle.

As I opened the front passenger door of his cruiser to sit down, I noticed a small brown teddy bear in the front seat between the trooper and me. I closed the door and handed the requested items to the trooper. His bad demeanor was still very obvious, and I did not appreciate it at all.

Finally, after looking at my CDL license and realizing that my address was listed as a post office box in Madison Heights, VA, he rudely commented that he knew that I didn't live in a post office box. He wanted to know my physical address. As I started to respond, I picked up the small brown teddy bear. Law enforcement officers sometimes keep these toy bears in their vehicles to calm down and comfort small children at accident scenes.

I placed the bear next to me while I rubbed its little head and began telling the trooper that I did not have a physical address at this time and usually slept in my truck. Or I slept at a local motel when I was back in the city where my company was located. He should have let it go at this point. But he didn't.

"Do you have a family?" he asked. I replied, "No."

"Why not?" he continued.

"I was raised in an orphanage," I replied, "and don't have any close family or many friends."

Again, I will repeat he should have let it go. But he didn't.

Now don't forget that this is near Christmas. Usually, this is the time for most people's families to unite for the holidays.

"What will you do Christmas Day?" he asked.

"I will get a motel room, if I can find one, and hope that maybe a restaurant close by will be open so I can eat and sleep," I responded.

At this time, I stopped rubbing the little teddy bear's head and placed my arm around it. As I pulled the little teddy bear close to me, this did not go unnoticed by the overly aggressive state trooper. I noticed tears in his eyes, and he was having a difficult time with his speech.

I know that some will say that I did all of this intentionally, and maybe I did. But I was pleased with the change in the trooper's attitude and certainly with him giving me just a warning ticket. Thanks, little teddy bear.

Driving for a local company in Madison Heights was something I did for a year. The money was good and visiting all the New England states was a treat.

I was once lost in Connecticut and stopped in front of an office building to ask for directions. As I entered the building, I noticed that four ladies were sitting at their desks working.

I introduced myself and asked if they knew where a particular place was, and they all looked up as I continued speaking. After completing her directions for me, the lady asked if I would stay and talk to them for a while longer.

This seemed a bit strange, but I am a nice man and asked why. The ladies started laughing and told me that they had never met someone who spoke like I did. It was my Virginia accent. So just to have some fun, I said, "Much as I would like to, I better mosey along." It was worth it.

When I would arrive back in Virginia either on a Friday or Saturday, I would check in at Harvey's Motel in Lynchburg to rest and clean up. Then I would sometimes go to the Marine Corps League on Lakeside Drive. Once in a while, I would go to the Hilton to dance.

One particular night would change my life forever. As soon as I walked into the Hilton, I noticed that it was crowded. It was a typical Friday night, and as my eyes adjusted to the dim lights, I caught a glimpse of a stunning lady. She had beautiful teeth that were being highlighted by the above strobe light. She was wearing a flowing dress and flat shoes, and she was dancing with enthusiasm.

It was pure attraction for me, and as soon as that dance was over, I wasted no time at all in arriving at the table where she and her friend were seated. It might have been a little presumptuous of me, but I just knew this lady was the one I was looking for. She reminded me so much of the ideal wife, a vision I had formulated in my mind and was seeing brought to life.

I asked her to dance, and we did until the Hilton closed. I walked her into the foyer and asked for her phone number with a promise that I would call.

The following day, I did. We met at King's Island Restaurant for lunch, and afterwards, we went to a movie at Candlers Station.

From that moment on, we spent time together whenever I was in town. This went on for quite some time, until I broke up with this beautiful girl.

Perhaps the breakup was due to a guilty conscience on my part, or maybe I still wanted to try and "clean up" the past somehow. But in several months, I knew that I had made a serious mistake. I called this beautiful lady that I had met at the Hilton, once again, and asked her out.

I held my breath until she answered with a "yes." Judy and I dated about five years and were married in 1998.

-Judy's Brief Story-

This is told by her, so that you can know her a little better.

I was born and raised in the Allentown, PA, area. My parents moved around a lot, and I attended several elementary schools and three different high schools. I felt no allegiance to any school and was pretty much a loner.

After attending a business school in Bethlehem, PA, for two years, I became an executive secretary. My following job was working for a wholesale lumber company for three years until I married my first husband.

I had met my husband at one of the clubs in Allentown where my friends and I hung out. He was in his senior year of college and later attended dental school in Philadelphia, PA. We were married right before his second year of dental school. I was able to procure a job as an executive secretary to the executive director of Temple University Hospital.

One year after moving to Philadelphia, I gave birth to our first son, and we began to find out how dire our situation was. Things were tight.

After my husband graduated from dental school, he, our son, and I moved to Buffalo, NY, for his three years of training to be an oral surgeon. Our second son arrived two weeks after our arrival in Buffalo. Two years later, our first daughter was born and one year later I was pregnant again.

After three years, my husband had to fulfill his military obligation, and we all moved to Shaw Air Force Base in South Carolina, where our second daughter was born. The two years went by quickly and we had to decide where we would settle.

We looked at several locations. A friend of ours from the Air Force base who had moved to Roanoke, VA, called us and said that there was a need for an oral surgeon in Lynchburg, VA. We took a trip to Lynchburg, met a lot of nice people, and decided to relocate there. We moved in July 1974.

On May 18, 1975, our second son was hit by a car and died. This was the most horrific year of my life. Trying to overcome the emotional pain led me to taking some art and photography classes. I found them comforting.

We decided to have another child and our third daughter was born in February 1977. My primary focus was being a mother to my four children.

I was able to take enough classes to graduate from Lynchburg College in 1993 with a Bachelor of Arts degree. Besides obtaining a communications in arts degree (BA), I also minored in journalism. I began doing freelance photography and graphic design.

Unfortunately, my marriage didn't last. We were separated in January 1992 and divorced in June 1993.

One day, a friend asked me to accompany her to a class she was taking at the Hilton Hotel. There was a dance at the Hilton every Friday night, so we decided to go in. We had no idea how crowded it would be.

I was experiencing a somewhat melancholy mood, but when a certain redhead asked me to dance, that all changed. He was telling tales so unbelievable and funny that I had to laugh. He asked me to meet him for lunch on Sunday at King's Island Restaurant. Jackie and I started talking, laughing, and dating and it wasn't long before I knew I was falling in love.

Jackie was the most thoughtful and affectionate man I had ever met. We married on February 6, 1998.

Chapter 17

(Judy)

After Judy and I became involved, the desire to see more of each other increased exponentially. We planned to remedy the situation.

Why did I pick that night to go to the Hilton in Lynchburg in 1992, and why was the most beautiful girl I'd ever seen there? I usually did not go to the Hilton, and neither did Judy.

When I put into perspective the good things that have happened to me in life, out of the clear blue, this night tops the list. Meeting Judy that night has brought me the most happiness of anything I can remember. And in my mind's eye, my wish to meet a girl that looked like Judy was deeply embedded, long before it happened.

We hit it off immediately, and she says to this day that I made her laugh with my tall tales. I danced as I'd never danced before while holding her close as I dared. That whole time, it was clear that she was very intuitive and nobody's fool.

She had class, and when I asked for her phone number at the end of the evening, I was so relieved when she gave it to me. The next day was our first date, which included a meal, a movie, and a dared kiss. We became attached in a way not spoken but known.

My life from this day forward would change, and I knew it and prepared myself for the love I needed to give and was open to receiving. It was finally natural for me after a lifetime of searching and hoping.

We worked together and supported each other with everything we had to offer. We put it all on the line and knew it would succeed.

Judy began looking at ads in the paper so I could change jobs, hoping to find one which would allow us to spend more time together. It was not long before she noticed an ad from Brink's, Inc. on Fifth Street in Lynchburg. That's all I needed to know.

I gave my notice to my employer and applied at the Brink's office for the position. It was just a few days before I was hired part time. Becoming a full-time employee meant awaiting a background check.

My job was to assist the head cashier in the office as well as assist on the armored cars when needed. It was a job I enjoyed until I was offered a salaried position sometime later.

There was a problem with my background check that caused a problem with my being hired full time, and it had to be corrected. My record reflected that I had taken a car when I was sixteen while living at a children's home in Salem. As the law stated, that incident should have been expunged on my nineteenth birthday, providing I had not been in any further trouble. And I hadn't.

I called the Virginia attorney general's office in Richmond and explained the situation and was informed that I needed to hire a lawyer. Then I received a call back from a lovely lady who said, "Jackie, you don't need an attorney," but she did not explain exactly what action to take.

Judy and I talked about it, and she went to the library to research the Virginia code. After we were confident we were correct, I decided to write to Bill Clinton and Janet Reno, the President of the United States and the United States Attorney General, respectively. It was a short time later that I received a letter from the United States Office of the Attorney General, acknowledging my letter.

We waited almost six months before the FBI office in Washington, DC called to inform me that my juvenile record had indeed been expunged. They further stated that the Virginia state police had been notified.

I was then hired full time at the Brink's office in Lynchburg and soon was offered the head cashier's position. This meant becoming a salaried as opposed to hourly paid worker. I accepted.

I would work for Brink's for five years before deciding yet again to try another exciting career move. This one would be the most enjoyable job I ever had other than being a military policeman in Annapolis. And this next job would indeed turn into a career that lasted over twenty-four years.

Judy and I are different and thank God for it. We are not bored, since we have so many things that we share that bring us anticipation and excitement. We have genuinely enjoyed and learned much from each other.

Judy supported my ideas and encouraged me when we started our investigations business. She patiently waited until I returned from long workdays, many miles away, in different states and many locations within those states. I appreciate Judy so much for her help getting the business off the ground.

Several years before Judy and I married, I dedicated my life to Christ and asked for a chance to live a life pleasing to Him and asked for help in cleaning up my life. I no longer wanted to drink, smoke, or gamble. I wanted to be able to commit myself to my future wife. I stopped the vices overnight without any regrets at all.

Judy and I were together for about five years before we married, and we were both convinced that she was making the right decision to become my wife. We are still convinced twenty-four years later.

This wonderful woman has helped me accept my past, embrace it, thank it for its lessons taught, and release the parts which no longer serve. This is a daily process, one which I sincerely hope we all, as humans, aspire to do.

-Our Kids-

I have one child, named Becky, from my second marriage. She is highly successful in all aspects of her life. She has a wonderful husband, mother, and two beautiful daughters. I'm so proud of her and the woman she is.

Judy had five children. One is deceased. But we, as a family, have become a rather large group, particularly at the holidays and especially at Christmas.

Judy's children are also successful and have been extremely nice to me. Kerry, Debbie, and Melissa are very attentive to their mother. Melissa has been especially good to me when I needed her help with transportation to the hospital for a medical procedure. Her willingness to stay with Judy while I was in the hospital is also very much appreciated.

Chapter 18

(Self-Employment)

I do not drive a red Ferrari, nor do I have a pretty girl on each arm. But I have spent the night at a Holiday Inn Select with my beautiful wife while traveling in a green Corvette.

In 1998, the year we were married, the decision was made by Judy and me that my next adventure should be something that I would enjoy. So we explored the idea of me working for myself.

Judy is my biggest fan, and we loved planning my next move. One day, she asked what I thought of private investigators. I told her that since I had been watched by a couple over the years, the subject sounded interesting.

I immediately attended a four-week, private investigator's training class and finished first in my class. I was on my way.

My first opportunity came when I learned that a former deputy, still employed with the same department but in a different position, was planning to retire soon. He also wanted to start a company and become a private investigator himself. I made myself known to him.

We met, and we made real progress in our plans immediately. This still employed county worker would own the company. I would be the lead investigator, and Judy would design the brochures needed for us to introduce ourselves to the legal community.

We were off to a great start as work came our way, and I was happy with the income. But after a while, I knew that I would be much more successful owning my own investigative business and doubling my income.

I informed my friend, who owned the company I was presently working with, that I was starting my own investigations business. In less than a skinny minute, I had my business license and met all the requirements to start Beacon Investigations, LLC, in 2002.

Judy was very instrumental in helping create my company logo, stationery, business cards, brochures, and doing any other marketing requirements. She also understood that I would be away from home for long time periods in various states. She immediately started making musical CDs for me to help pass the time when driving long distances.

At this point, I had about four years' experience as a PI. I became friends with two other former police officers who had also started their businesses, as well as many others who were former FBI, ATF, and state police employees. There were others, both men and women, who became professional acquaintances and had also gone into business for themselves.

On the first day of officially being open for business, one of those friends sent me three cases in one day. I became blessed with many opportunities.

I'll say from the start that my favorite people to work cases with are females because they are much smarter than men, don't have anything to prove, and can talk their way into or out of most investigative situations that prevail. In my experience, I'll take one female over two male investigators, any day of the week.

Now there were exceptions, and I worked with a younger male PI in Lynchburg who was phenomenal in every case he and I worked on together. We both had a few differences in our thinking and in our techniques, but this worked to our advantage. I will refer to him as Kevin, but he knows who he is.

I worked mainly in Virginia, North Carolina, and Tennessee. But Virginia has reciprocity agreements with

North Carolina, Georgia, Tennessee, Oklahoma, Louisiana, and Florida.

In this new business, I was beginning to make more money than I ever had before and immediately purchased two surveillance vehicles to add to the one I started with. I also bought equipment, and a lot of money was spent on advertising and printed materials. I even had my own 800 telephone number.

Channel 13 in Lynchburg interviewed me twice, and that helped with business. During this time, I met some of the nicest people you could ever imagine.

But there were some not so friendly folks that I had to contend with too. I was cursed, threatened, shot at, and chased, on several occasions.

I was in a witness room one day in North Carolina with a man that I had been doing surveillance on during an adultery case, and he asked me if I was the investigator that had caught him and my client's wife together. Of course, I said, "Yes."

He then began to inform me that he had better not catch me on his property and that he was friends with a state trooper. My response was, "I'll stay off your property if you stay off my client's wife."

-Road Rage-

This story takes place in Chattanooga, Tennessee. It would involve working with another private investigator documenting an affair that my client's wife was having with a delivery driver. She was an attractive person and mild-mannered as far as we could tell, but this assessment would change radically in just a short time period.

We had driven most of the night before setting up surveillance at her apartment complex. This location was where she was living during her separation from her husband.

My partner this day was a retired police lieutenant from a big northern city, and he was very apprehensive about southerners. His outlook was going to be justified very soon.

He felt that folks from the South were very deceitful because of being so friendly. He was suspicious of them avoiding contact with others unless attending church or needing something. I'm only telling you his viewpoint.

We had arrived and gotten into position when "Skippy" arrived happily on the scene. This man was literally skipping down the sidewalk like a child at recess time. Larry and I had two-way radios in our vehicles, and we were laughing so hard I could almost hear him without the radio.

We were on-site for about an hour, from when Skippy arrived until he left. He did not appear to have the same energy level that he previously had upon arrival.

After Skippy left the area, we waited until my client's wife left her apartment to ensure we had an excellent up-to-date picture of her. She soon appeared and walked towards her vehicle, but not before noticing my vehicle had a Virginia license plate.

She and my client lived in Virginia at one time, so it was no surprise that my license plate would attract her. She then quickly got in her car and headed to my location across the street. Larry was laughing. I was not.

As soon as I could move to the driver's seat from the back seat, I started my engine and headed to the two-lane highway with her in close pursuit. Upon looking in my rearview mirror, it was plain to see that her sunny disposition had changed dramatically.

I knew that if that woman attacked me physically, it would hurt. I did not want to have to defend myself and possibly hurt her, so I chose to try and avoid a close encounter with her.

She drove up to my passenger door as we were traveling at high speed. With her window rolled down, she screamed and cursed at me.

I stayed in the left lane so I could hopefully catch her off guard and turn in the opposite direction. My plan was to stay on the two-lane road and avoid stop signs and red lights, if at all possible. After a few minutes of being chased, I saw that Larry had caught up with us and was directly behind her vehicle.

It occurred to me that if I turned at crossovers and drove in the opposite direction a couple of times, she would give up the chase. I informed Larry of my plan, and he got ready to follow me.

We made the turn and headed in the opposite direction, and that put Larry behind me with her on his rear bumper. It was my turn to laugh, and I did.

I told Larry that I would peel off at the next exit and try to get away from her in town. I did exit the two-lane road. This time, she decided to stay on Larry's bumper. He called me about thirty minutes later and told me he had finally lost her.

On the way back to Virginia, we stopped at a Shoney's. During our meal, and after we finished laughing, I asked Larry what he thought of southern folk now.

Larry was a good man and not given to talking badly about people. He certainly was not a man that used cuss words often. But that day was different!

As of this writing, I am semi-retired because I don't want to leave my wife for long. But I do from time to time assist other investigators with research and locating missing people. There are many stories I can entertain you with, but I am bound out of respect for my clients and innocent people to not do so.

160

Chapter 19

(Life Goes on)

-Haywood and Milton-

Change is inevitable. Nothing is permanent.

In early 1992, Haywood's health took a turn for the worse, when he had a stroke, and his life changed dramatically. But before the stroke, around 1980, I noticed differences in him.

When I paid him and my uncle a visit, unannounced, the conversation began with all three of us understanding our relationship dynamics. After all said and done, we had grown to respect and trust each other.

I realized that there had been times when all three of us had helped each other, despite difficult beginnings. And I let it be known that I was there to adopt them both as my dad and uncle, no paperwork needed. Having already adopted the Cunningham name, the transition should be easy.

My uncle Milton laughed and said, "Hell, I thought you always were our boy."

And he was correct since I had always called Haywood "Daddy" and referred to Milton as my uncle. I didn't feel comfortable calling them anything else, but I still never felt at ease until later on.

There were many times in my life that there were no real connections with anyone. I was lonely, surrounded by so many people, and not belonging anywhere or to anybody.

Before this day, we all three had changed, and it was just understood without words that we cared for each other. On the day of my visit, I needed to say and hear it.

They were pure country and didn't hold back when they had a thought or something to convey. Daddy once asked me how I had so many women, since I "weren't that good looking."

My uncle said, "Haywood, it ain't his looks. It's his ways."

My dad taught me to shoot and was the first to teach me to drive a car. He called me once, after I became an adult, and told me he was going to buy me a BB pistol and rifle, since he had not done so when I was a child.

He never let me down in a time of need and let me borrow money if necessary. I remember he often said, "By jingo."

Haywood also served in the Army during WWII. He was a strong man.

Milton was a lady's man who played the guitar and fiddle. No one knows how many children he fathered.

My uncle loved Neosporin. He thought it was a miracle ointment. He also loved strong spirits, and he chewed homespun tobacco.

I'm reminded here of another story about getting what I deserved. My uncle and dad loved to laugh and once they found something worthy of a good laugh, they would repeat the story for years to come and laugh uncontrollably. That in turn would make the audience laugh.

I've always been very curious about things and have on many occasions found that some things are best left alone, such as my uncle's homespun tobacco. People called this tobacco "twist."

Well, it was hanging on a nail in my upstairs sleeping area and after days of looking at it, I felt it was time for me to give it a try. I twisted off a small chunk and placed it in my mouth, as I had seen my uncle do on many occasions.

I did not find it to be very enjoyable. After having swallowed a small amount of the tobacco juice, I went outside to spit out the rest of the tobacco from my mouth. That was my plan.

Just before getting to the yard, a sickness I never ever experienced or could possibly imagine came over me. Spitting was not necessary as I became deathly ill.

I dropped to my knees, and in my inexperience, pleaded to God to spare me. He did spare me, but not before I felt like I was on a merry-go-round that was out of control with no stopping in sight. Holding onto a nearby rose bush did not help either! There were moments when I thought I was upside down, looking down from the sky. This was better known as a hallucination.

Not sure how long I was in another zone, but as I slowly recovered, it was fairly certain that my tobacco chewing days were over. It was all these years later, while discussing homespun tobacco, that my uncle offered some to me.

He had just purchased the tobacco, and his offer for me to have a try at it prompted me to tell the story. Dad started laughing and didn't stop for several minutes.

This would be brought up for the rest of my life. I did actually enjoy them telling the story and was glad to be the subject of their entertainment.

He could hang his tobacco anywhere he pleased. I made a promise that it would be safe from me.

Note: Swallowing chew can lead to nicotine poisoning. Nausea, vomiting, dizziness, tremors, sweating, rapid heart rate, and seizures are all symptoms of nicotine poisoning. Nicotine can poison through ingestion, skin, eye, or mouth contact, so always safely store tobacco, and dispose of all chews. (Cleveland Clinic, 2022)

Milton would hurt you if you threatened him. He used the word "thunderation," a lot.

I will not relay some of the rather graphic details of what I mean by saying that Milton was known to seriously hurt some people. But this was in self-defense.

My father died in 2009, and the following year, my uncle died. I had put them in a nursing home after their health had deteriorated, and I visited them and saw to their needs as much as possible. Occasionally, I would take them out to visit their home place or go to the drug store.

And the thing that meant a lot to me after I placed them in a nursing home, was as I was leaving, after a visit with Milton, he stood up and hugged me and told me that he loved me. He thanked me for taking care of him and his brother. And they both were most welcome.

-Mamie-

"My man done learnt to make billfolds!"

When I was a young lad living in Gladstone, a fair amount of my kin were sent to the Virginia State Penitentiary located at 500 Spring Street in Richmond, Va. They were incarcerated for various activities which included murder, moonshining, robbery, stealing billy goats, and a whole host of other unlawful activity.

No one was surprised when one of my kin was transferred from the Amherst County or Nelson County jail to 500 Spring Street for an extended stay behind bars. Do not confuse this type of stay with Extended Stay America Hotels.

Now let me get to the funnier part of this story. I remember once, when I had a short visit with my mother, it appeared to be a special day for her. She had received a package from her imprisoned husband.

In the package was a handmade men's leather billfold, most commonly called a wallet these days. My mother's husband wanted her to sell the item and send him the money. This would enable him to purchase tobacco and snacks.

I'll never forget her saying, "My man done learnt to make billfolds." I was witnessing her enthusiasm over this new revelation and remember thinking that making leather goods in prison must be a good thing. She was so proud.

My young life may not have been a bed of roses, but it did not lack in entertainment! I seldom recall any of my kin trying to be funny. They just were.

Whenever I could throughout my life, I would visit my mother and give her money and small gifts. But even though I had compassion, it was uncomfortable for me, and I would leave after a short visit.

My mother always felt that I didn't love her, and that was true, in a way. She wanted me to love her as children love a beautiful, nurturing, and devoted maternal figure. I saw her as none of those things.

I truly had compassion for her. I always wanted a mother with whom I could communicate and do things that would make her proud, as any child would want. I would imagine.

At times, I would visit one of my brothers that I liked, and we would go riding and talk. He and another brother and sister were still living with my mother and her second husband.

Once, when I took my brother home, we discovered that our younger brother was in the house alone and crying. Upon further inquiry, I learned that my mother's husband had beaten my mother in front of my younger brother and had taken my mother next door.

I stopped talking and went to the house next door and confronted my mother's husband, asking him if he beat my mother. I could tell that he had, but he denied it.

Just after his denial, I immediately started beating the hell out of him and in the process, broke his nose and caused as much pain as a fist beating would allow. It was during the time that I was attacking my mother's husband that I wanted her to realize that I loved her in my own way.

I was protecting her. I do believe that she received that message, and I am confident that her husband received it.

Mamie had a rough start and lived a rough life, which caused me considerable pain and grief. Nonetheless, I absolutely loved her, in the best and only way I could. She passed away in 2006.

-Annie and Craig Megginson-

Never underestimate the faith and knowledge of a country girl. This story was written and told to me by my grandmother, who was the daughter of Annie and Craig Megginson.

My great-grandfather had lung cancer in 1907. After the doctors had given up hope, my great-grandmother stated the following: "You shan't die. You will let me put a lye poultice on you."

My great-grandfather said, "Do anything you want to do."

She drew some new ashes from the open fireplace and poured cow manure over them to make what she called a lye poultice. She spread the mixture on a cloth and laid it under the painful lung. Then she gave him a heavy dose of whiskey.

Almost from that hour the pain and suffering subsided. The lump disappeared, and little more than a week later, my great-grandfather walked out onto his little farm a healed man.

I am only telling you this story as it was relayed to me. It is in no way meant to be medical advice.

He lived for twenty-four years after that and never had any more trouble with his lungs. He died in 1931 at age seventy-nine. Annie died in 1953.

Chapter 20

(Siblings)

I am the oldest child and half-brother to eight siblings. Seven children were born to Mamie and two were born to Robert by his wife.

We were all born in either Gladstone or Amherst County. Coming back to Virginia in 1968, I would become familiar with my three siblings that my mother had during her second marriage. I liked them and would occasionally see them.

They had endured a hard life, and I will not expound upon any of my relationships with them except to highlight a memorable moment or two. I was reminded of how blessed I was to live in the children's home.

The oldest of these three was named Murphy. Naturally, he can't speak for himself, but he left a memory that I'll always keep in my heart. I loved him.

I immediately took an interest in him and gave him several vehicles over time to enable him to go to work and to have a vehicle that was paid off. He was actually very funny and loved to laugh at silly stuff. He was also a good guitar player.

He and I would sit and laugh at a song by John Conlee titled "I Don't Remember Loving You." The lyrics suited us, since we had failed marriages, and the song was hilarious to us.

While visiting Murphy one day, I noticed a bathtub on his porch, and I asked him what he was going to do with it. He then took me to his bathroom to show me where he planned to place the tub.

I immediately realized that the tub was much too big for his small doorway and inquired as to how he planned to bring it into the house. He took me to the porch where the bathtub was and pointed to a gasoline chainsaw.

He said, "If that thing will start, I'm going to enlarge the door opening." That sounded logical to me.

Murphy was always a quiet person. If he had been given a chance in life and had some education, he could have done most anything.

He loved living alone and once built a shack out of pallets. He lived in the woods, in this shack, next to a creek on River Road in Madison Heights for about two years. I finally convinced him to come live with my wife and me when I lived on Martins Lane, also in Madison Heights.

He would just stay in my basement and sleep without any initiative to do anything else. I thought for his own good, I would ask him to leave, in hopes that he would put some effort into helping himself. This strategy worked.

And for a while, he really changed and even found a house to rent. He purchased a motorcycle that he loved to ride, and he played music.

In 1997, Murphy bought a 1980s red Pontiac Fiero that I absolutely liked. He offered to sell it to me, but I already had three vehicles and really did not need it.

Sometime later, he called me and asked me to visit him at his home, so Judy and I went. As soon as I arrived at his house, he came outside and handed me the title and keys to the Fiero. Of course, I asked why.

He said, "Because you like it." I tried to pay him for it, but he refused.

As jovial, entertaining, and fun to be around as Murphy was, he fought severe depression, off and on, for most of his life. I found out that he had even spent time in Beaumont.

On September 9, 1998, I received a phone call from my sister, Betty Jean. She informed me that Murphy had died by suicide.

In addition, a sister named Virginia, and a brother named Michael have also passed away. I have five remaining siblings as of this writing.

-Malcolm-

I always laugh when my brother tells me that my hairline is receding. I always tell him that his will one day as well!

In modern society, the saying, "Blood is thicker than water," is used to imply that family relationships are always more important than relationships with friends. Not necessarily.

Malcolm and I met as kids when we lived at the Virginia Baptist Children's Home. We became friends instantly and have maintained our friendship for sixty-two years.

We did everything together. We worked in the fields at the home to grow food. We milked cows, got up hay, fed the pigs and did everything else we were told to do. Plus, we chased girls, and sometimes we caught a few. We weren't told to chase girls, but we figured we would just do it anyway.

After completing our chores at the home, we would go to downtown Salem and rake leaves, shovel snow, cut grass or do anything anyone would let us do for money. We would acquire enough money to take a girl to the movies from time to time.

We also purchased our own clothing with the money we earned. Washing and ironing what we worked for was important. There were so many kids at the home, and we did not want our clothes lost or worn by anyone else. We wanted to look nice, or stand out, in a manner of speaking.

We laugh now about how protective we were over our personal things. And we laugh now about trying to figure out how to protect what little hair we have left.

Malcolm was and still is my best friend. When I had my hip surgery, he took care of Judy and me by doing things like cutting our grass. He said that he didn't want me to hurt myself.

After I was able to cut my own grass, Judy and I agreed that Malcolm really enjoyed taking care of our lawn. Since he is retired and his wife died a few years ago, I asked Malcolm if he would like to continue with this task. He agreed, and I pay him, of course.

Malcolm and I drove down the streets in Salem, a few years ago, just to see how the lawns looked. We had not mowed them in over fifty years.

Surprisingly, they appeared to be well maintained. We always thought we did the best job!

Even though I lived in different towns and states after we left Salem, we ended up in the same community. It has really been a treat to be able to see my "brother" again on a regular basis.

Chapter 21

(My Biological Father)

My mother made sure that I knew who my father was. Robert Wills was the first cousin of Haywood Cunningham.

Robert served in the Navy for a short time. After leaving the military, he was known for having a wide variety of skills in construction and repair work and eventually worked for the C&O Railway in Gladstone.

Even though I had known Robert all my life and was sure he was my father, this was never discussed by the two of us. We favored each other, and I was invariably referred to as Robert on many occasions by my uncle Milton. Other people in the Gladstone community also commented regarding my looking like Robert.

I am not sure what the circumstances were, but I remember when my biological father, his wife, and their daughter, lived upstairs in the big house where my great-grandmother lived. This is the same house I had been living in as a young child.

There were times when Robert would see me alone, and he would give me comic books. I enjoyed the pictures but was not able to read yet. I don't remember when Robert and his family moved from the upstairs room.

Much later in life, I owned a Chevrolet Corvair that needed repair. Robert had one that was not being driven, so I stopped at his house and asked if I could purchase the part I needed.

He didn't say much but walked to his parked Corvair and removed the part that I needed. He then repaired my Corvair. Robert was not a talker, at least not to me.

After the repair was completed, I asked him how much I owed him. He said nothing and simply walked away.

It was odd behavior, but much later in life, when he was in a nursing home, he would always tell me to visit him whenever I wanted to. I am not sure that I ever really got to know him, and I know for a fact that he really never knew me. He was Robert, and I was his biological son, not much more or less.

In 2009, after Robert was placed in a nursing home, I would visit him, and we would talk about a variety of things, but never my paternity. This would change, a short time later, when one of his daughters asked if I would consider having a DNA test performed. She and about everybody I knew suspected that Robert was indeed my biological father.

Naturally, I had to bring this up with Robert, and he was opposed to it. He stated that he didn't understand how it was possible that he could be my father.

I am not one to entertain stupidity for an extended period unless it's me being stupid. You see, Robert had married, and he and his wife subsequently had two daughters. One was named Mary Ann, and it was she who was curious about the DNA test.

Soon after she spoke with Robert about taking the test, he agreed to participate. A short time later, the results came in.

It was clear, based on the results, which were 99.996 percent positive, that unless a miracle had taken place, Robert Wills was my biological father. And I didn't take the time to explain to him how his being my father was not only possible but undeniable.

Soon after the test, I assured Robert that I was not in favor of referring to him as "Dad" and certainly did not want him to reference me as a son. There was no need for this.

My goal was to get to know him and help him in any way possible, simply as his friend. I would bring him things and occasionally take him out to eat.

Once, while waiting for a restaurant to open and sitting in the car, I made eye contact with a lady sitting in a car parked next to us and smiled. She then exited her vehicle and walked up to my door and asked me if I knew her.

Of course, I didn't, but we had a particularly good chat until the restaurant opened. I gave her my business card as I usually did to people I'd met for the first time.

Robert would witness this type of behavior on my part several times in different environments, and one day he made a statement to me saying, "Looks like you are picking out your next wife." That was not the case at all, and I explained to him that I was a very sociable person at this point in my life and enjoyed talking to people.

He was never convinced of this and even told my sister that he doubted my salvation because I had been married so many times. This made me laugh.

Once, during one of the many talks Robert and I had, our different personalities came up. I told him that even though we had a lot of similarities, our social skills were not the same, at all.

I reminded him that due to my instability as a child and being in so many different situations early on, I had to develop in ways that he never did. My survival and success were based a lot on my social behavior, and I admitted to enjoying this behavior more than necessary at times. And indeed, my behavior had led me to get involved in situations not conducive to good marriages.

I was not proud of my past antics and indiscretions, but I had promised myself that I would change. And I did.

Robert was never convinced, and this really never bothered me. I know who I am. So do most people who know my wife and me. Judy knows me better than anyone else.

But I enjoyed getting to know my biological father. I'm awfully glad to have spent this time with him. Robert Percy Wills died on September 15, 2012. He was eighty-three years old and had a military funeral.

I was asked by my sister if I wanted to be listed as Robert's son in his obituary. I told her I did not. But I requested to be listed as Mary Ann's and her sister Robbie's brother in Christ. And so it is.

Epilogue

-A Serious Love Affair-

I typically look at everything from a romantic perspective. Over the years of growth, I've found that my first love is still an intricate part of my life. Outside of my faith, she has been my friend and ally for an awfully long time.

I'm speaking of music. It has carried me through thick and thin.

I clung to it beginning at an early age of turmoil. Through living away from my roots at an incredibly early age, through the jungles of Vietnam, through several broken relationships and still onward, music is my friend. And yes, even in worship, it has been a friend.

This relationship began while living from pillow to post with relatives, sometimes mine and sometimes not, who had a guitar or a fiddle. These fiddle players occasionally had a good singing voice.

I was not always impressed with what I heard, even at an early age. After hearing a radio station in 1952 with the call letters KWKH in Shreveport, Louisiana, which produced the *Louisiana Hayride* country music hour, I knew this was my door to the music I liked.

After this event, I sought a radio everywhere I went, especially in any dwelling I might be in during the night. The nighttime was when you could pick up radio stations across half of the country.

In those days, we had tube radios with loop antennas. They worked very well if you placed your hand on the antenna itself and were careful not to touch one of the boiling hot glass tubes.

I soon discovered several different radio stations across the country that played country music. Two such stations were WCKY Cincinnati, Ohio, and WWVA Wheeling, West Virginia.

The late 40s and most of the 50s were the beginning of some of the earliest rock and roll and different exciting genres of music that would personally keep my attention. And I found that music, even in the best and worst of times, would conjure up emotions which only the person listening could identify and deal with.

Even though I still listen to a wide variety of music, I find that personally my taste has changed, and I tend to listen to songs that express love. I am also very fond of songs of praise.

To put it all in perspective while looking back over the years, I must say that music introduced me to a new world of enjoyment. Heck, I dare say it even introduced me to a new and better way of life.

References

- Winter, Milo. "The Aesop for Children: with Pictures." Rand, McNally & Co., 1919. Library of Congress. https://read.gov/aesop/143.html. Accessed 19 May 2022.

- Pullen, Steve. (2010). *Natural Bridge Juvenile Correctional Center Study.* https://rga.lis.virginia.gov/Published/2010/RD238/PDF

- Cleveland Clinic. (2022). Nicotine Poisoning. https://my.clevelandclinic.org/health/diseases/21582-nicotine-poisoning. Accessed 19 May 2022.